ANTHONY J BARBER was born in Stoke-on-Trent in 1962. While studying Architecture and Design to Postgraduate level in West Yorkshire, he sketched and painted both in Yorkshire and on visits to Scotland's west coast and the Hebrides. In 1994 he moved to Lewis, where he now paints full time, based at the Harbour View Gallery, a studio gallery just above Port of Ness harbour and beach. His paintings are in private collections in the UK, Europe, USA and Australia.

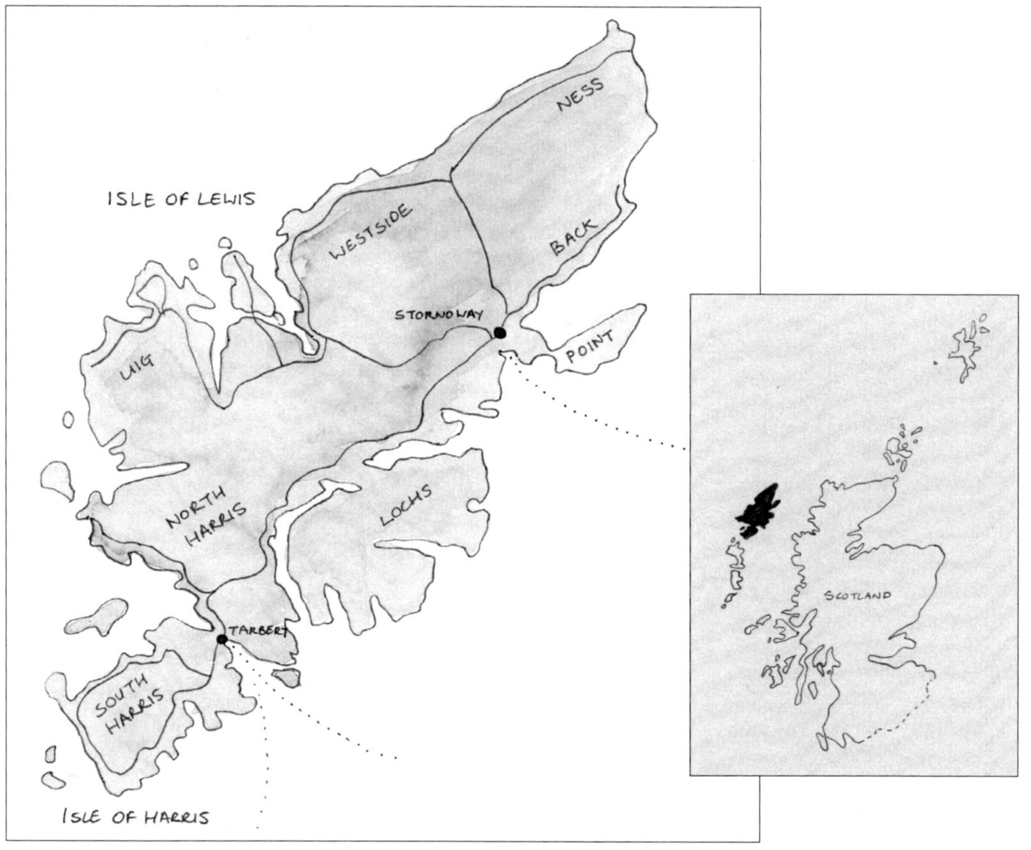

ISLE OF LEWIS
NESS
WESTSIDE
BACK
UIG
STORNOWAY
POINT
NORTH HARRIS
LOCHS
TARBERT
SOUTH HARRIS
ISLE OF HARRIS
SCOTLAND

Drawn to the Edge
A Lewis and Harris Sketchbook

ANTHONY J BARBER

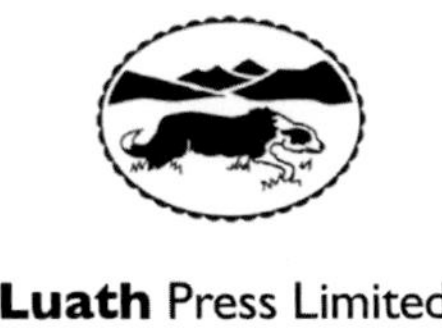

Luath Press Limited

EDINBURGH

www.luath.co.uk

First published 2018
Reprinted 2022, 2023, 2025

ISBN: 978-1-912147-63-2

The author's right to be identified as author of this book
under the Copyright, Designs and Patents Act 1988 has been asserted.

The paper used in this book is recyclable. It is made from low chlorine pulps
produced in a low energy, low emission manner from renewable forests.

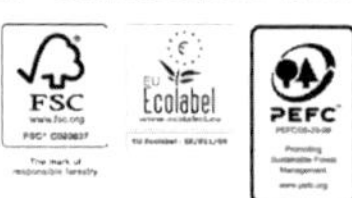

Printed and bound by
Robertson Printers, Forfar

Typeset in 11 point Sabon

© Anthony J Barber 2018

Contents

Acknowledgements

I would like to express my thanks to Gavin MacDougall and the team at Luath Press for help and guidance during the preparation of this book. Thank you to John Hawkridge, for being the first person to suggest that I should consider having a book of my work published. Thanks as well to anyone who has bought my work over the years as this has allowed me to keep doing what I love in a place that I love. To the people of Lewis and Harris who made us welcome from our very first day on the island I offer my heartfelt thanks. The reason why this is a good place to live has as much to do with the people as the place. Finally to Kate, Sophie and Annie. I couldn't do it without you.

In memory of my Dad
John Barber 1938–2016
For my three girls
Kate, Sophie and Annie
and my Mum

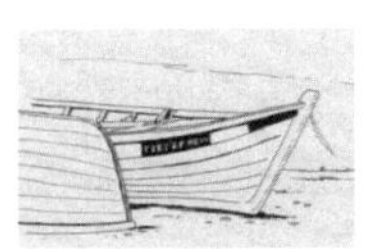

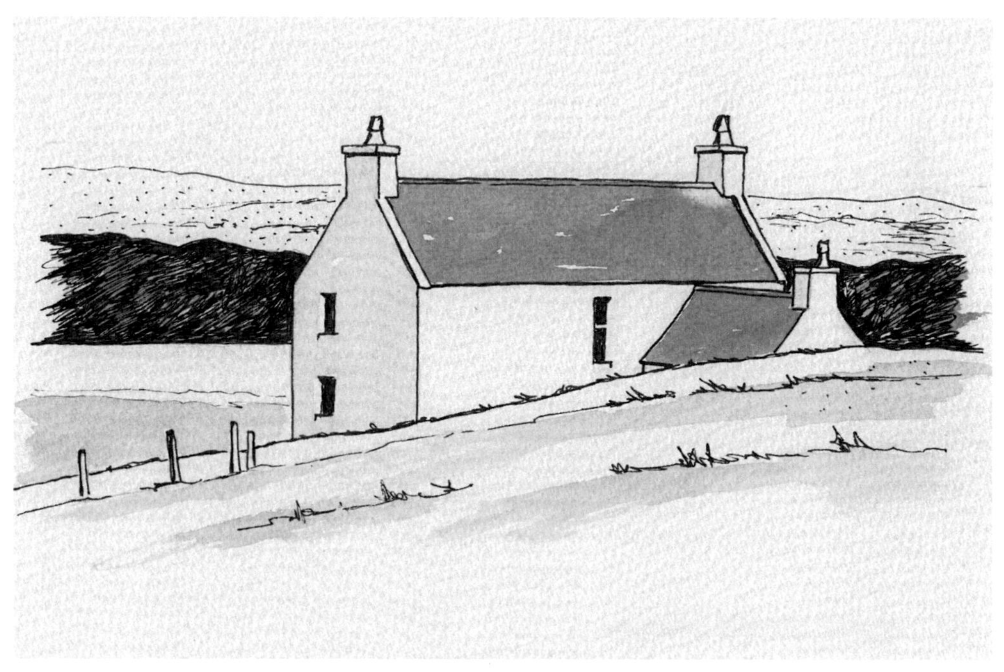

Above Port of Ness beach.

Introduction

WE VISITED LEWIS and Harris for the first time in summer 1990. Before leaving our home in West Yorkshire we made rough plans for the trip. Based on a study of an island tourist map which showed a vast beach at Uig in southwest Lewis, we decided that this would be the best place to spend our first night in the Outer Hebrides.

After a three and a half hour ferry crossing from Ullapool to Stornoway on the CalMac ferry MV *Suilven,* we made the long road journey to Uig to pitch our tent beside the pristine white sand, in the shadow of a range of impressive hills. Despite the fact that we did not arrive until after ten in the evening it was still light.

On that initial visit we spent a few days camping in locations which allowed us to take in as much as we could from each base. Faced with limited time, we had to prioritise what we wanted to see as we were aware that we were only just scratching the surface of such a large island. There are nearly 200 miles of road on Lewis and Harris, and the various and varied small settlements are spread out with tracts of uninhabited land between them. We covered many miles, usually having to make the return journey on the same road used to reach our destination. Circular routes were rare and the going was often slow, as there were a lot of single track roads to negotiate. However, surrounded by such spectacular scenery, with good weather and on this occasion very few midges, it was a perfect introduction to Lewis and Harris.

We had visited many other west coast islands before making our trip to the Outer Hebrides and liked them all, but here the sky seemed bigger, the scenery bolder and the colours brighter. We had daydreamed for some time about 'getting away from it all' by moving to a Scottish island and after that first trip to Lewis and Harris we knew that, if we were going to do it, then it had to be this island.

In the following years we made many more visits until Easter 1993 when we made the decision to stop dreaming and seriously search for an island home. Our only criterion was to find an old, characterful house near to the sea and in a good position to start a business. After much searching we found a house above Port of Ness harbour and beach, and knew straight away that it was exactly what we wanted. A type of clinker boat called a Sgoth used to be built in Port of Ness by the MacLeod family, who also built our house.

We viewed the place twice before making a formal offer. The first viewing was on a perfect July day and the second was in late October when the sky turned black and horizontal rain and hail sent us running for cover. We were not put off by bad weather. After all, stuck out in the Atlantic Ocean and on the western edge of Europe, we had to accept that the weather would sometimes be challenging.

When we told people that we were moving to Lewis we received some incredulous looks and on more than one occasion were asked where it was. Our stock reply was always 'top left corner on the television weather forecast map'. It was understandable that people had limited knowledge of the islands, which never had much press attention; what morsels did exist usually described them as continually windswept and lacking in facilities.

In February 1994, when we collected the key for our new home, it was calm and bright and felt like an early spring day. A few weeks later when the weather changed and the wind reached 75mph I cautiously asked my neighbour, 'Is this as bad as it gets?' He answered, 'That's just a breeze, a good day to dry your washing.'

On a number of occasions in the following years we saw – and felt – the wind reach 100mph and over, but there were also pristine winter days without a breath of wind or a cloud in the sky.

A combination of things make living here so appealing to me. The rapidly changeable light and four-seasons-in-a-day weather have a lot to do with it, together with dramatic scenery which includes mountains, moorland, lochs, sea cliffs and unsurpassable white sand beaches. However, Lewis and Harris are more than just dramatic scenery and wild weather. In the weeks before we moved here, we did wonder if the hospitality we had received as tourists would change once we took residence, but the warmth of welcome, help and guidance we experienced from our very first day on the island was remarkable. An old-fashioned sense of community still exists here, and will hopefully continue to do so for a long time to come.

I have drawn and sketched since an early age and I still enjoy it now. Since moving to Lewis, my Hebridean sketchbooks have provided me with valuable reference material for many of my paintings. Before I start to paint I always look through my sketchbooks to see if any of the pictures inspire me. Sometimes a sketch can remind me of the day it was done, and based on that it may influence the colours and mood of the painting. However, some of the sketches do not make it to the finished painting stage, and were never intended to; they just record what I have seen and some of the places I have visited.

When I sketch, I work quickly to record the scene as accurately as possible, focusing on the details which I feel are important to the scene. Most of the sketches are ink drawings, some with the addition of a simple wash of watercolour shading. I use disposable, waterproof and lightfast ink drawing pens which come with various nib sizes. Sketching outdoors in the islands can sometimes be a cold, wet experience and I have to admit that there have been occasions when I have sketched from inside a warm car with the wipers on whilst the wind and rain pounded the roof. Collected here are some of the sketches made on my frequent travels around Lewis and Harris with some brief notes and recollections and some diary entries.

Anthony J Barber
Lewis
May, 2018

The symbols before and after my name have no meaning and are borrowed from my great uncle, who was a keen painter, and signed his own work in a similar fashion. A visitor to the gallery today takes a look at all of the paintings, studies the signatures on them and asks, 'Is this TAJ BARBERT a local artist'?

Diary entry: A movement catches my eye through the studio window. On the lane which leads up from the harbour, I can see a seal pup, obviously disorientated and quite a distance from the sea. I stop painting and rush outside to encourage it to turn back but the young seal is having none of it, showing its teeth to keep me at a distance. It is too big to pick up, and so the only solution is to barricade it in with planks of wood to stop it from going any further towards the main road. Eventually an SSPCA officer arrives, dons protective gloves and puts it into a cage and takes it away for a check up. Once given the all clear, the seal pup will be released back into the sea.

A Note on Lewis and Harris

LEWIS AND HARRIS, often referred to as two separate islands, are actually one landmass forming the northern part of the Outer Hebrides. Sometimes called the Long Isle, Lewis and Harris is the third largest island in the British Isles after the mainland and Ireland. The northern two thirds, roughly, is Lewis; the southern third is Harris. Perhaps the fact that the North Harris mountain range formed a natural barrier, which in the past could not be crossed, saw them treated as two separate islands. The arbitrary border runs roughly from Loch Resort on the west coast to Loch Seaforth on the east.

Sabbath observance is part of the culture. However, since 2009, Sunday flights and ferries to the mainland have been available and in Stornoway a few restaurants and one filling station now open on a Sunday. Outside Stornoway the vast majority of shops, visitor centres, petrol stations and cafes remain closed.

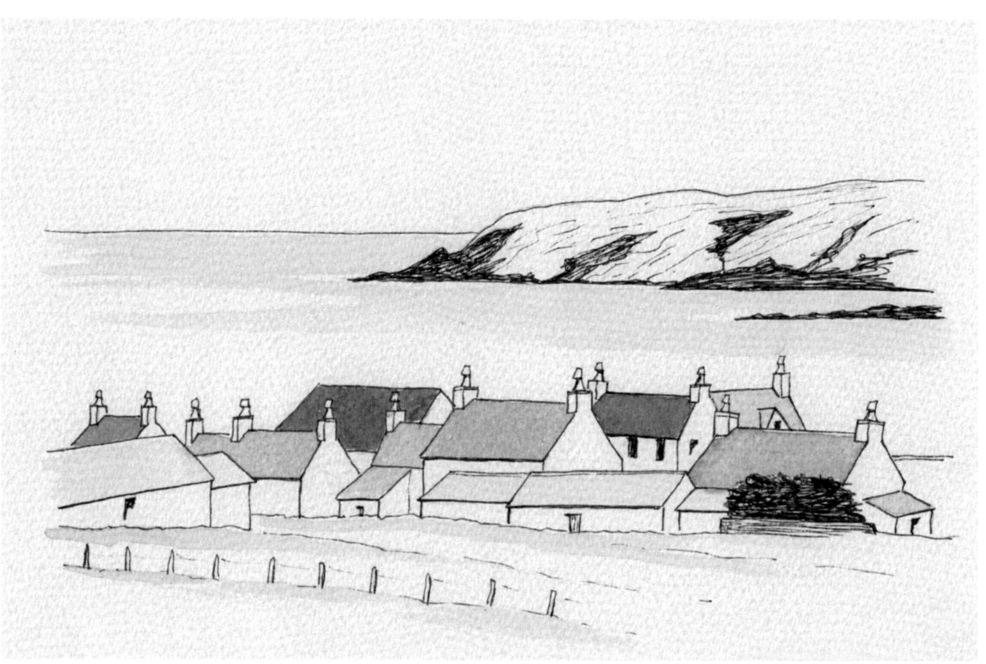

Port of Ness.

Ness

NESS, THE NORTHERNMOST district in Lewis, consists of around 18 small settlements. The name derives from the old Norse for headland, and many of the local place-names have a Norse origin. Crofting was the prinicipal way of life for many families and within living memory Ness was pretty well self-sufficient, with produce from both land and sea. Ness was once famous for its boat building tradition. Extensive stone and concrete walls protect the harbour, which is still used by small boats in the summer. Boats start to appear in April but are usually taken away again in October, before the worst of the winter storms begin and the sea crashes over the walls. The breakwater that marks the narrow harbour entrance takes the full force of the waves. As a result of the constant battering, it is now 3m shorter than when we first made our home in Port of Ness. The Butt of Lewis lighthouse, the most northerly point in Ness, and therefore in the whole of the Outer Hebrides, is one of the windiest places in the UK.

Diary entry: When we took up residence in April 1994 we had had a steady flow of visitors to welcome us to Port of Ness and to introduce themselves to us. One elderly man, who knew our house well from when he was younger, told us that he did not go to Stornoway until he was 21 'because you didn't need to'. He listed all the facilities which were once available in Ness and concluded by saying how people were more self-sufficient back in his youth.

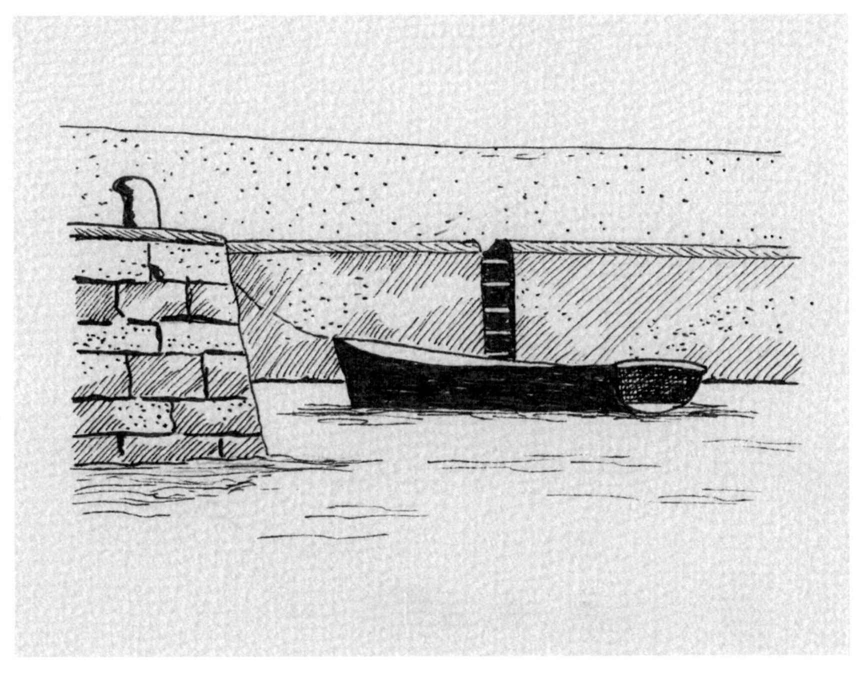

Harbour walls, Port of Ness. Constructed in the early 19th century, the harbour was improved and the breakwater built in the 1890s.

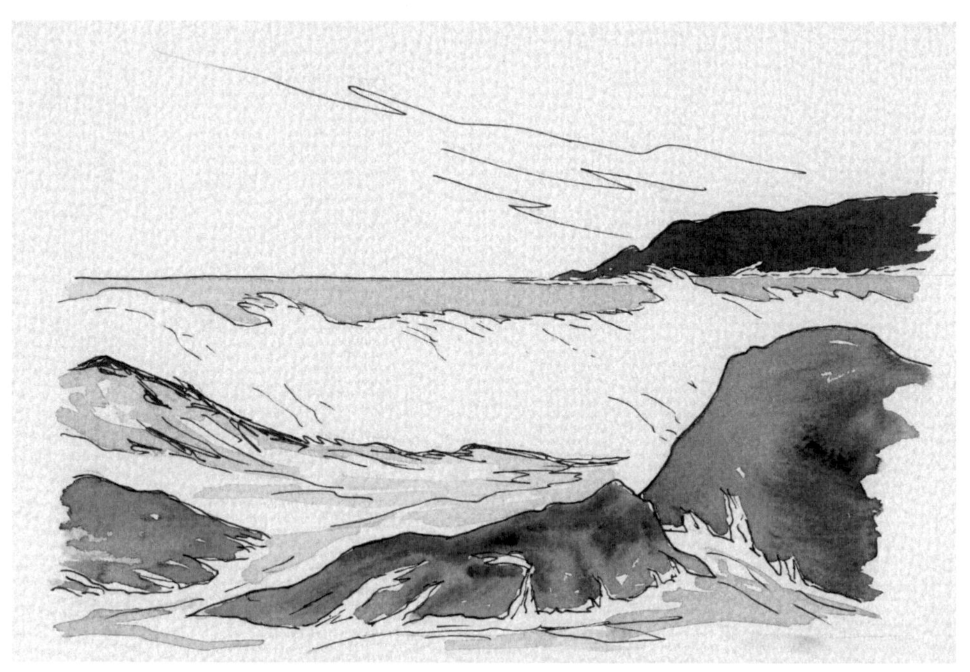

Breaking wave, Port of Ness.

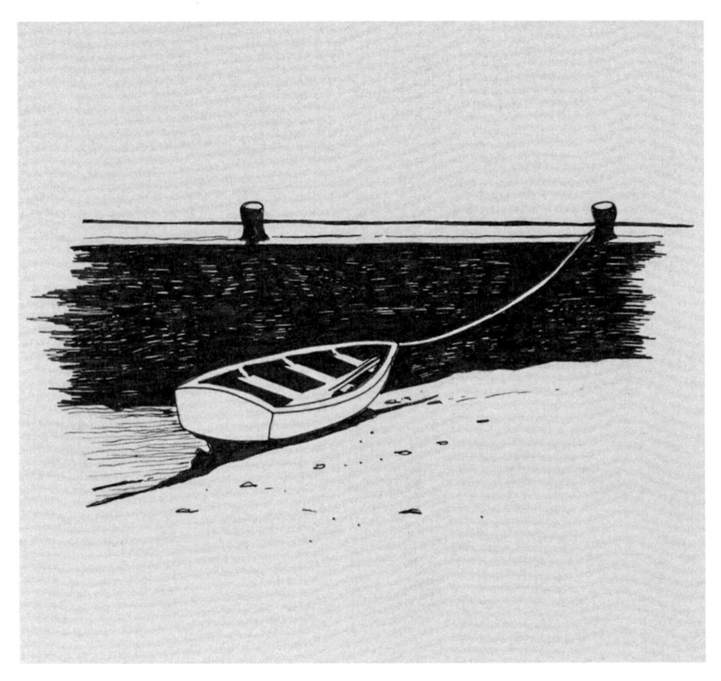

Beached, Port of Ness.

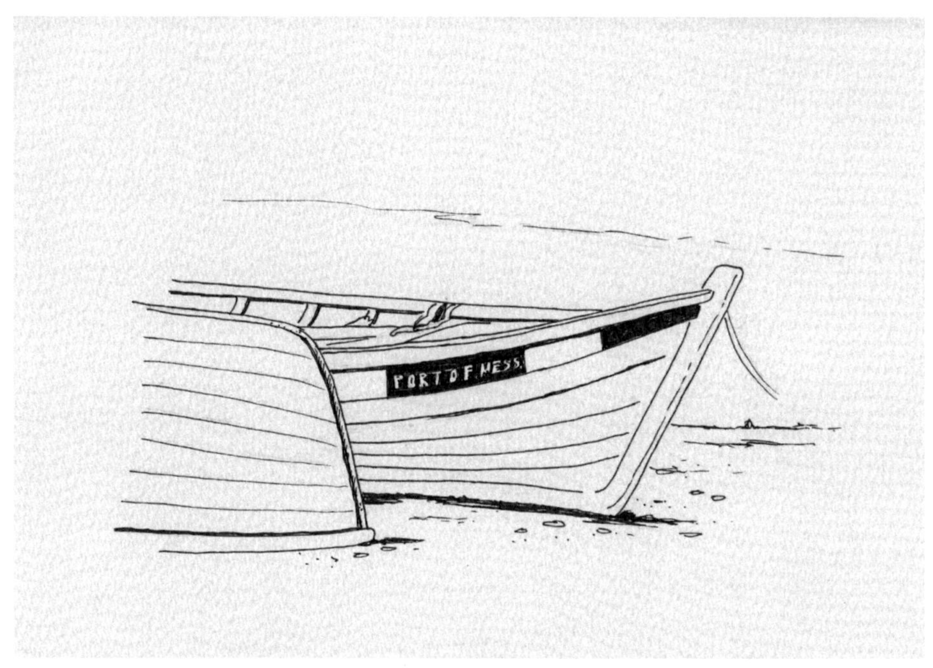

Boats, Port of Ness. A Sgoth is a traditional clinker boat built in Ness and used for line fishing.

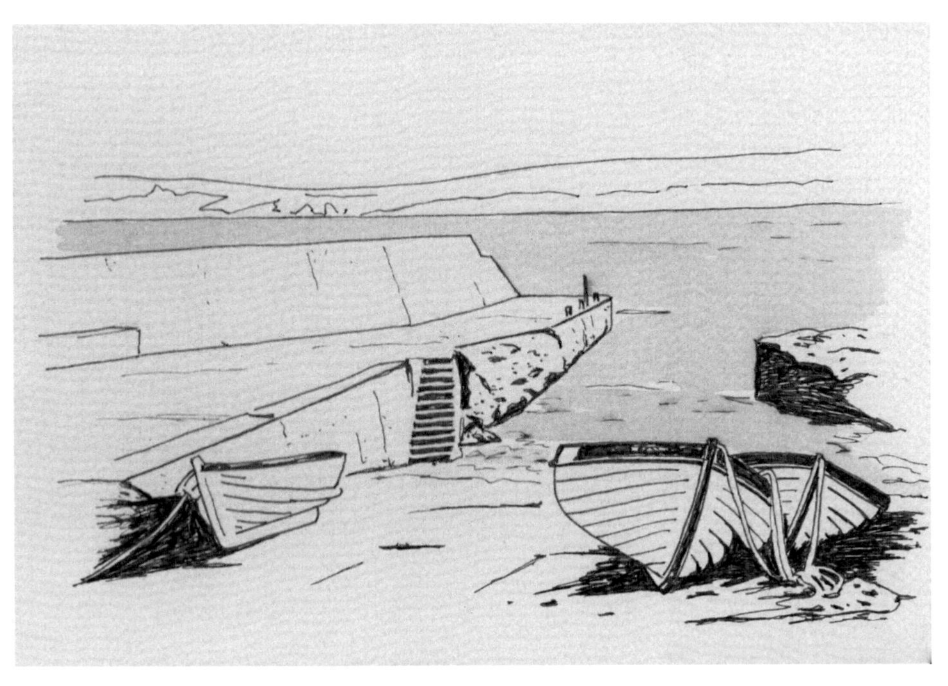

Breakwater, Port of Ness.

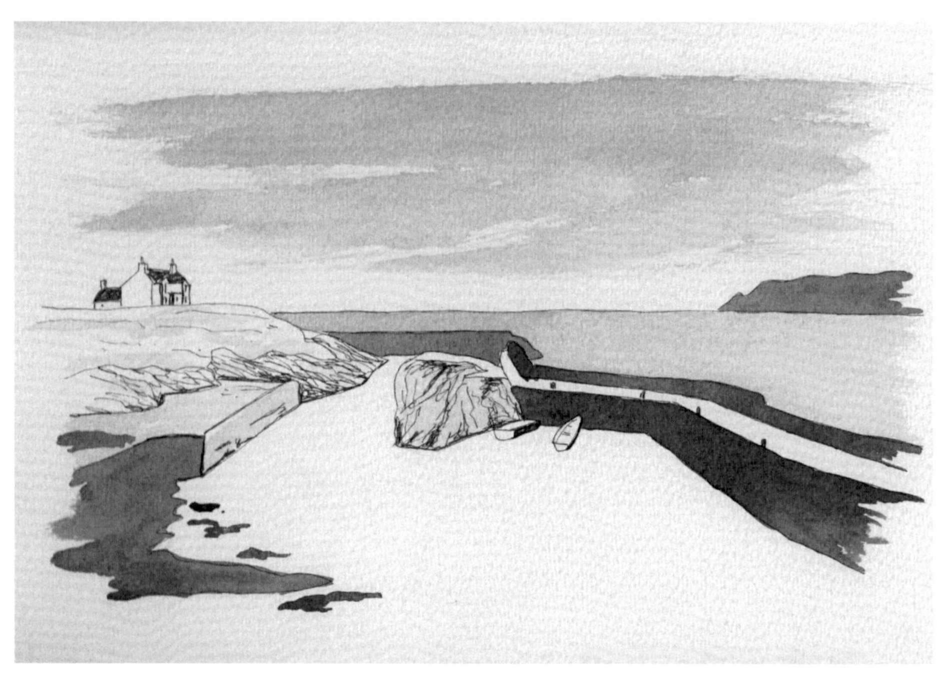

Low tide, Port of Ness harbour.

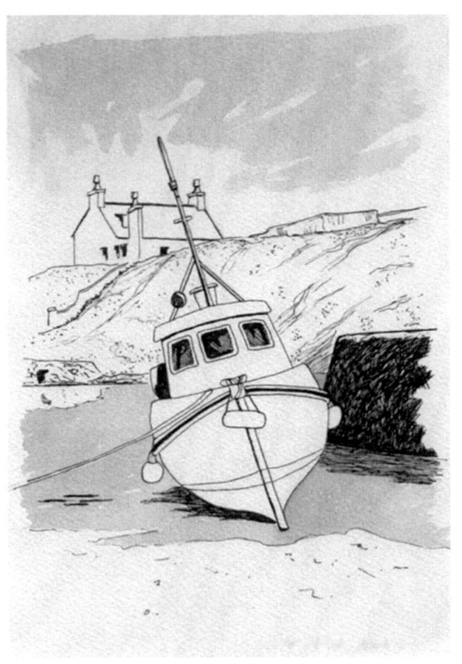

House above Port of Ness harbour.

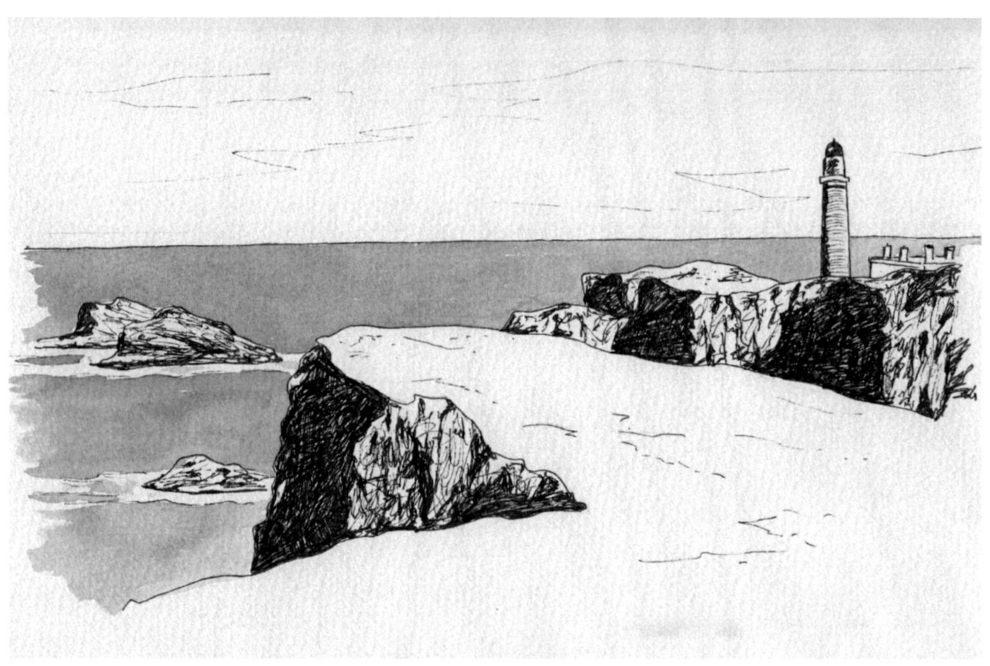

Sea cliffs, Butt of Lewis. The road north from Ness ends at the Butt of Lewis, then the sea takes over.

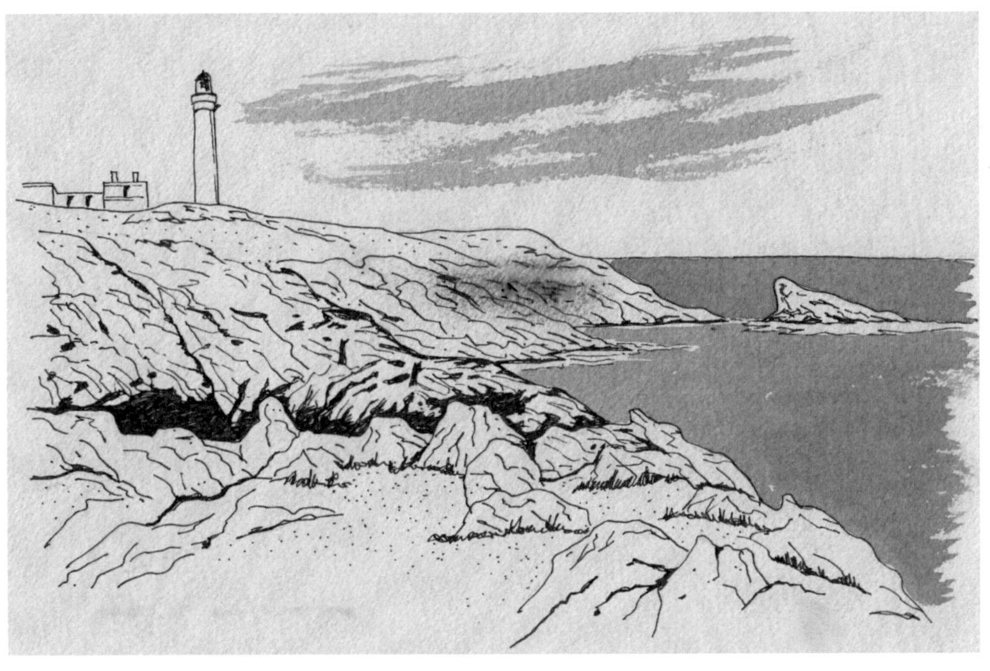

Butt of Lewis lighthouse. The climb to the top of its red brick tower is rewarded with a spectacular 360 degree view. It's like being on top of – and at the same time the edge – of the world.

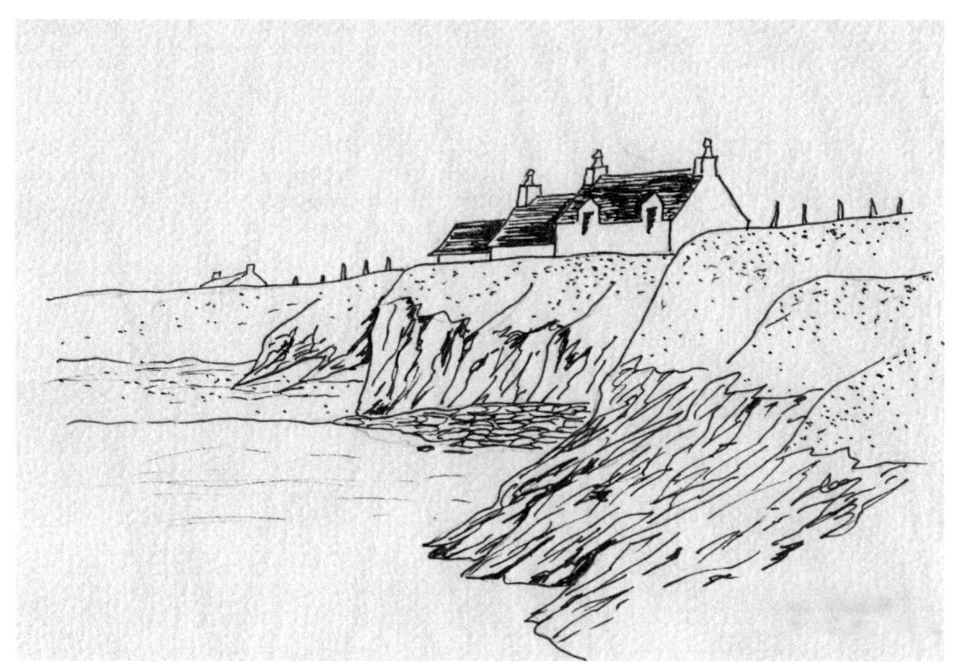

Port Skigersta, southeast of Ness, where ruins of 19th century curing bothies can be seen.

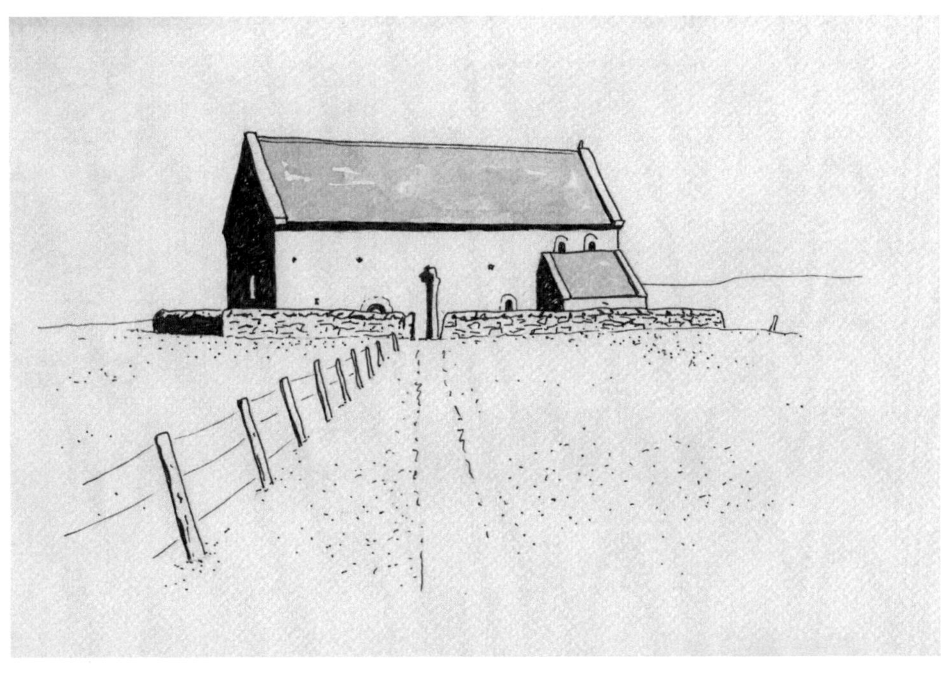

St Moluag's, a 13th century church in Eoropie. Traditionally known as a place of healing, it is also linked with Seonaidh, god of the sea.

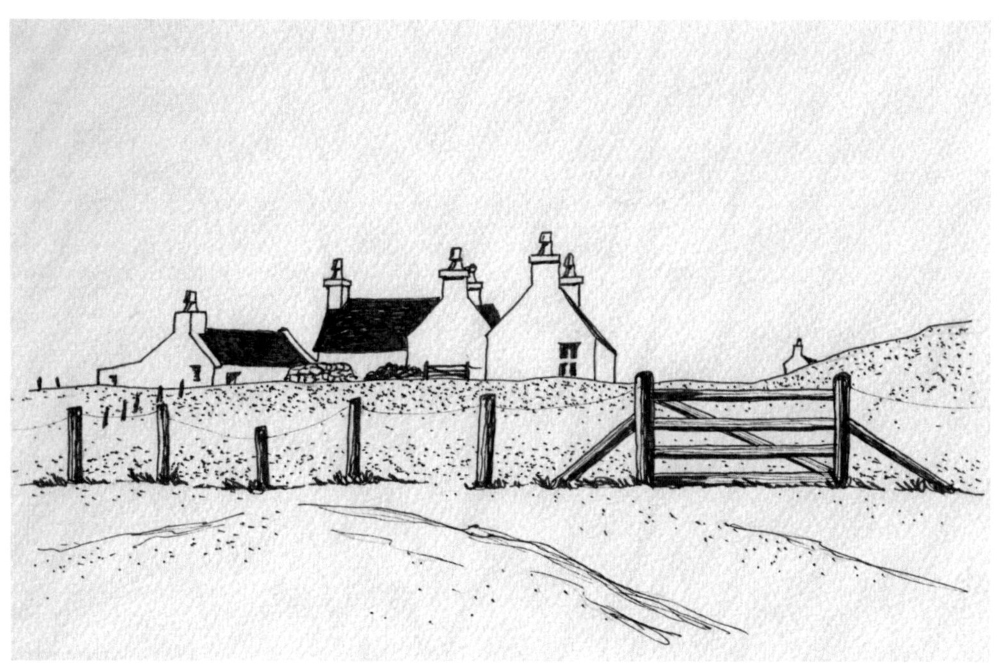

Crofts in Eoropie, the most northerly village in Lewis.

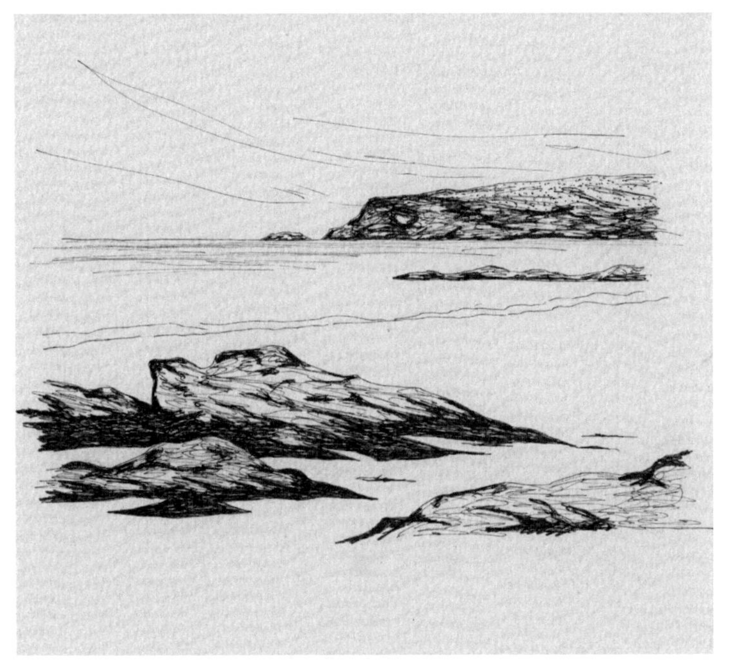

Eoropie beach, just south of the Butt of Lewis.

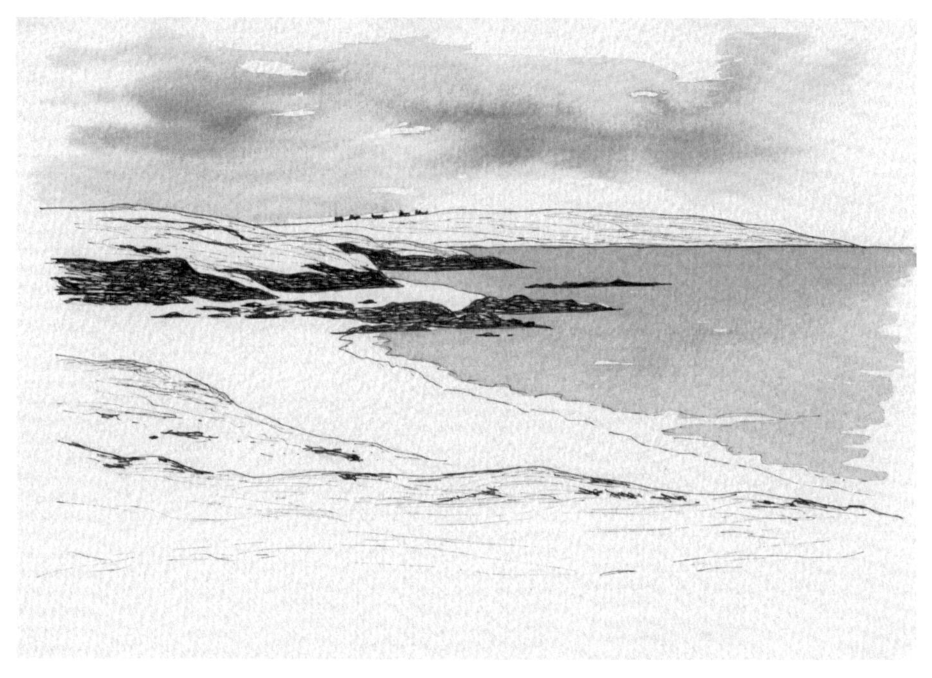

Swainbost beach. Near Swainbost are the ruins of the church of St Peter.

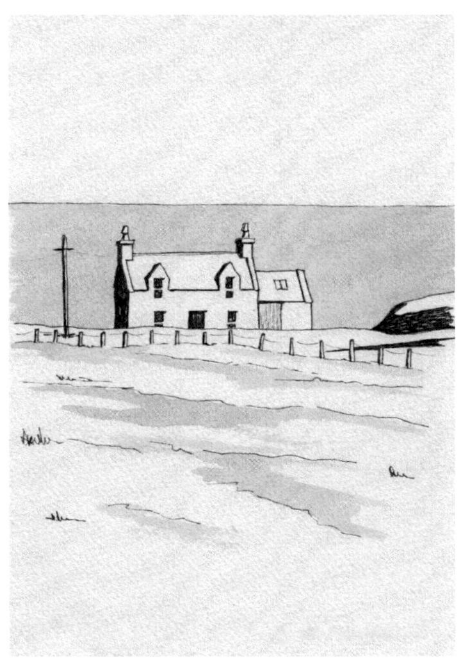

A croft house at the cliff edge, Eorodale, turns
its back to the sea and the view.

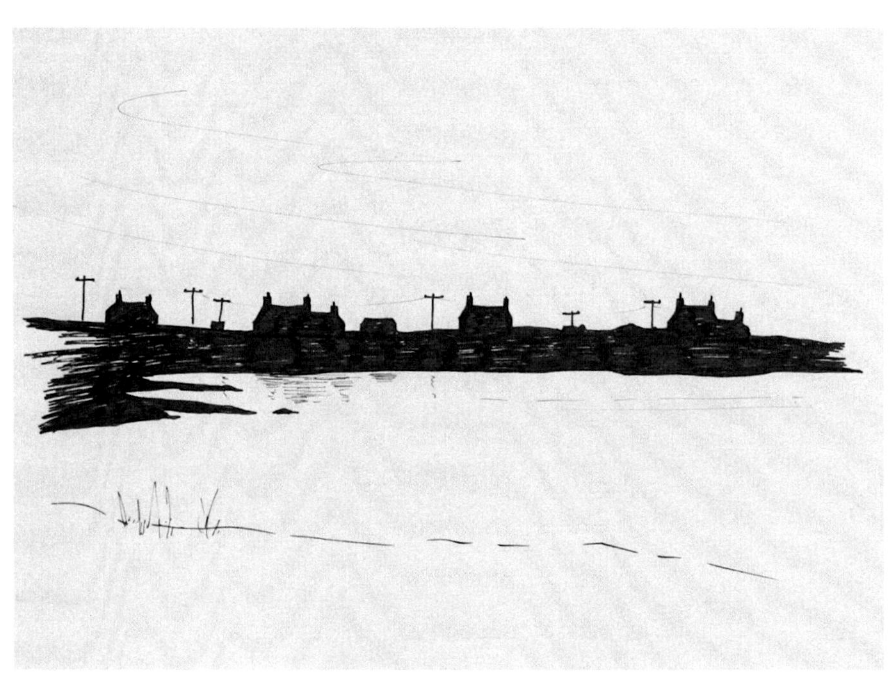

Crofts by the loch, Shawbost.

West Side

ON AN ISLAND rich in history and archeology, the West Side has some of the most important attractions, Callanish Standing Stones and the many historical sites making the 'West Side circular' a popular day trip from Stornoway.

Settlements are strung out along the coastal fringe from Ness to Gaynahine. Beaches and coves hidden from the road can be reached down single track roads; in contrast to Harris, Lewis keeps many of its beaches hidden and you need to work a little harder to find them.

Some islanders still cut peat from the moor for domestic fuel. The peats are cut with a spade and then thrown on top of the bank until they are completely dry, then they are taken home and formed into a peat stack. The smell of burning peat, once a typical Hebridean scent, is now, sadly, quite rare. The very first time we brought our own peats home from the moor, I asked a neighbour how many months' worth of fuel we had. Four months at best, he reckoned. After all that effort, I had hoped he might say we had enough for a year!

Conversation overheard at Callanish Visitor Centre.
Tourist: 'I don't know how you put up with all the rain you get here.'
Islander: 'We don't call it rain, we call it liquid sunshine.'

Diary entry: A stormy weekend for the time of year with all island ferries cancelled due to the weather. From the news we learn that an oil rig has washed ashore at Dalmore. It was being towed by boat en route to Turkey to be dismantled, when it broke free and ran aground on the west coast of Lewis. Luckily there is no oil spill, but you do have to question why it was out at sea when poor weather had been forecast for over a week.

(It took over two weeks for the rig to be safely refloated and towed 54 miles around the top of the island to the relative shelter of Broad Bay.)

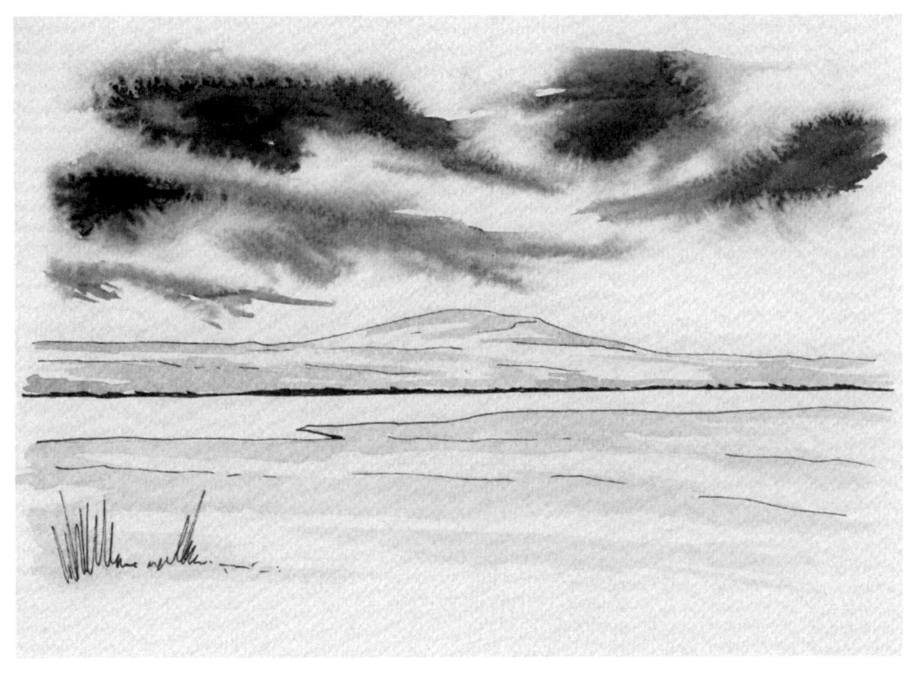

Barvas moor. Visitors to the low-lying west side often comment: 'There is so much sky here.'

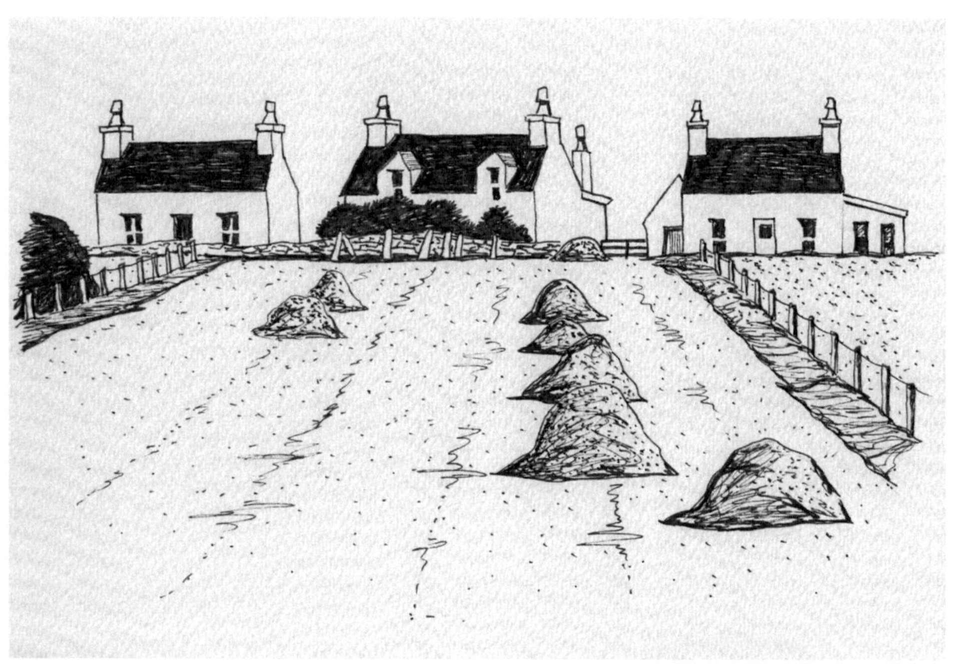

Crofts and haystacks, Borve. The North Lewis war memorial is in the village of Borve.

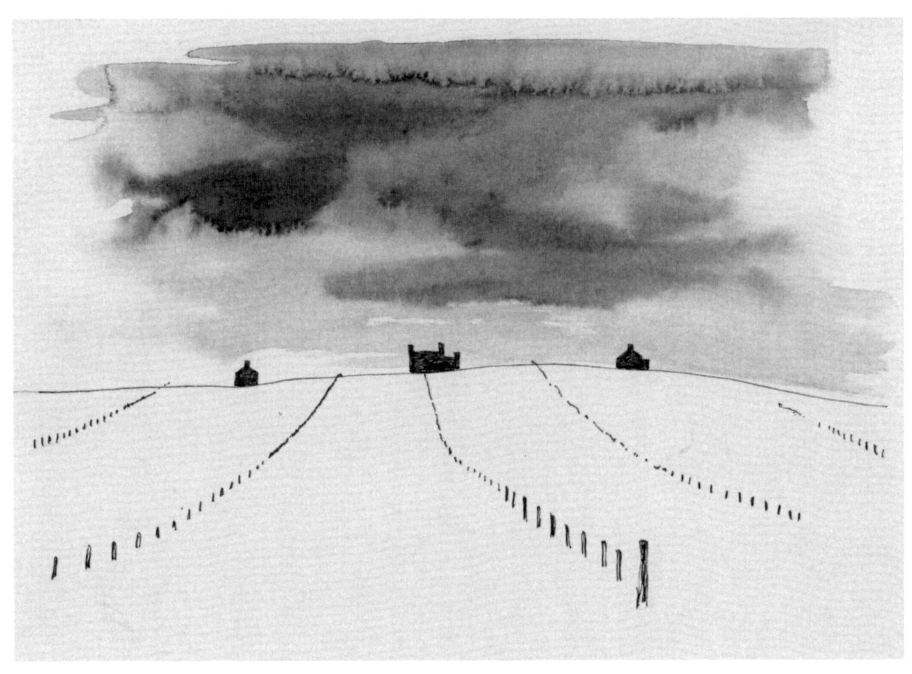

Traditional crofts laid out in geometric strips.

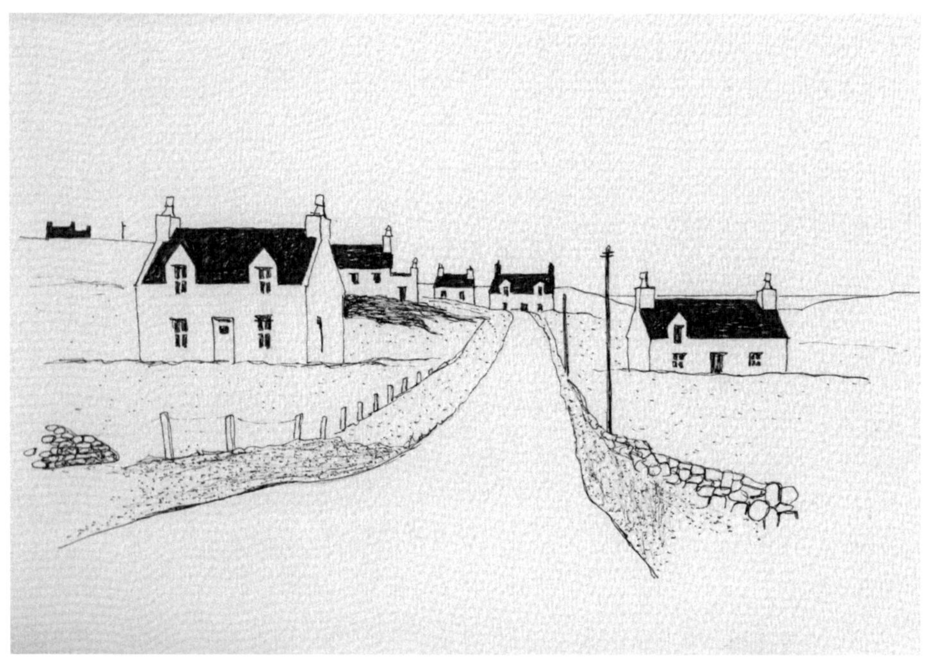

Galson.

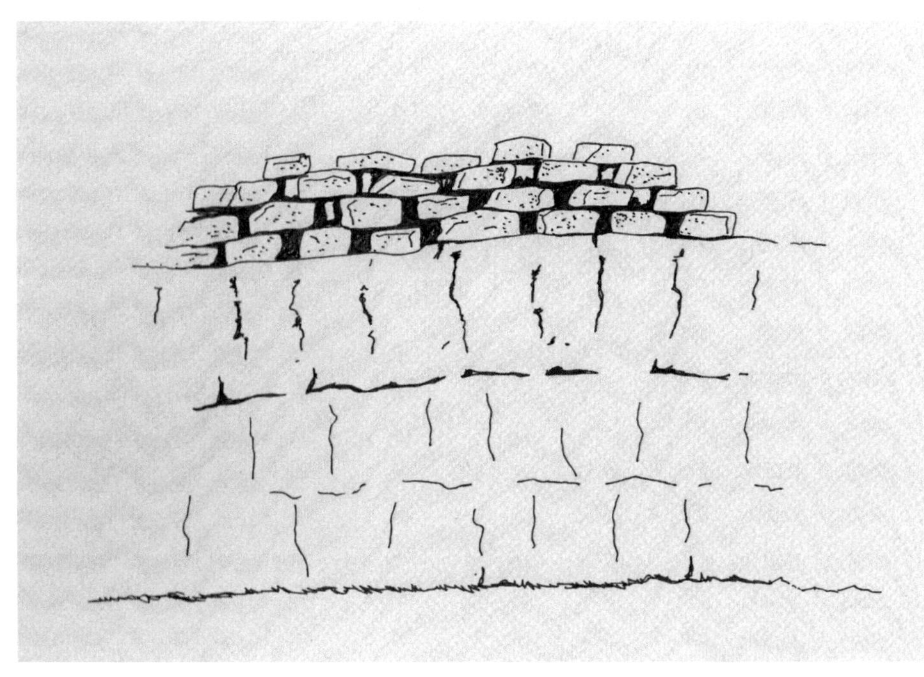

Cut peats drying on a peat bank.

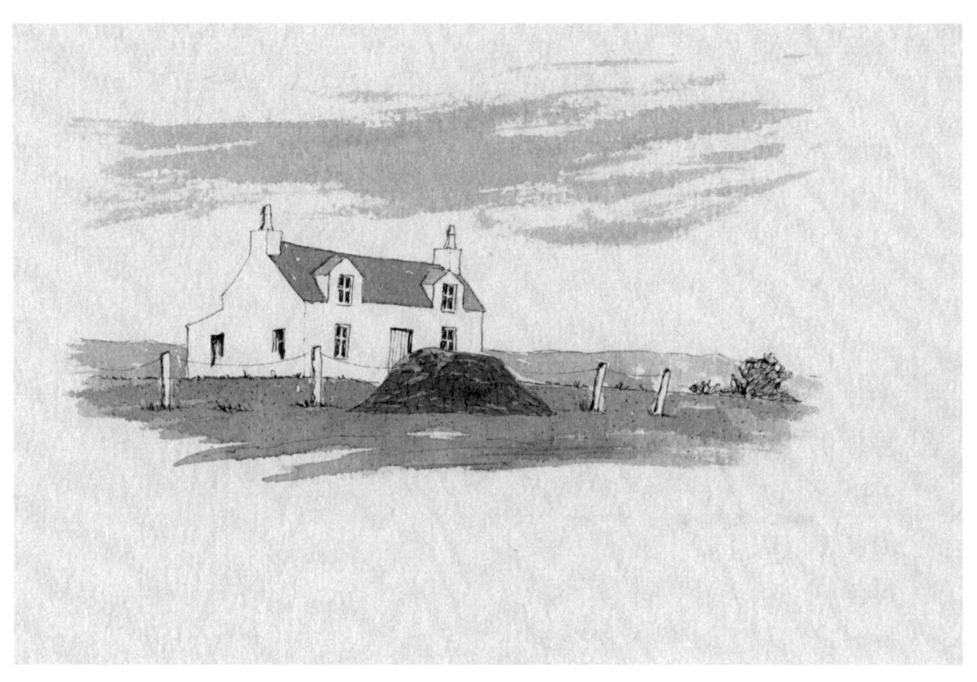

Croft and peat stack, Borve.

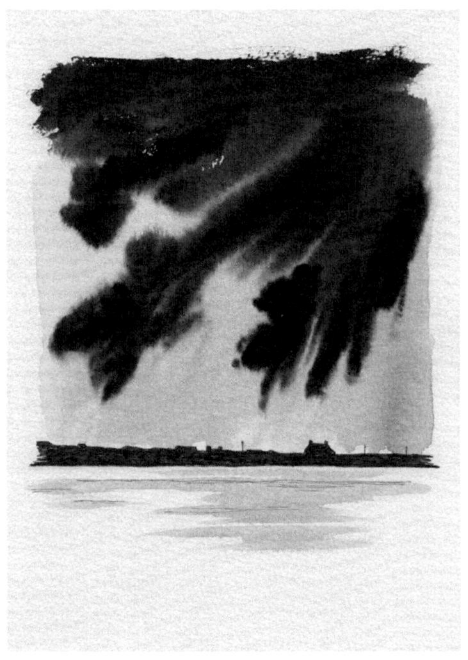

Wide open spaces, vast skies, storm clouds
gathering in the distance.

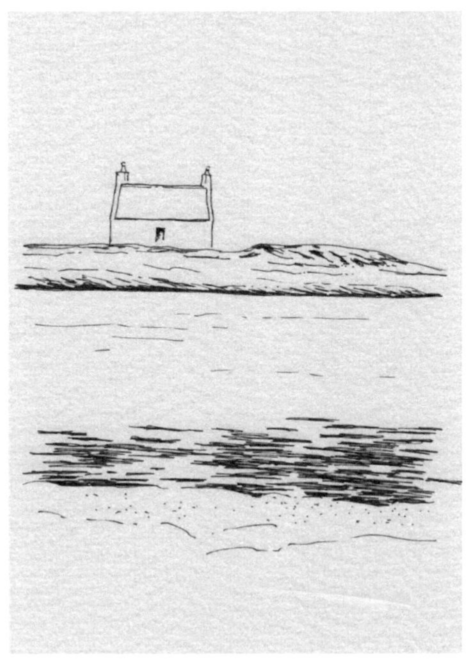

Loch Roag, known for its abundance of
shellfish.

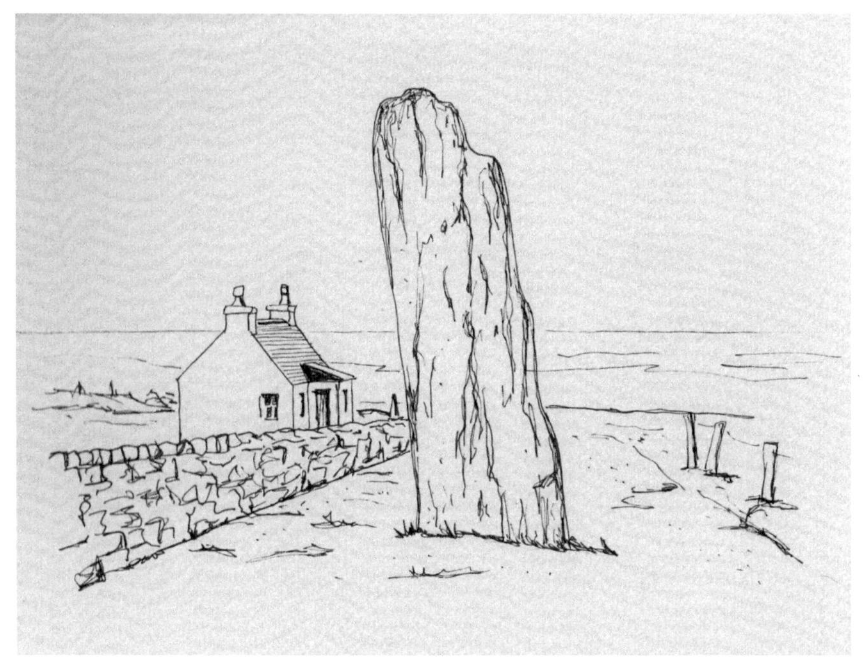

The Trushal stone, a single monolith in Ballantrushal, dating from the same period as the Callanish stones.

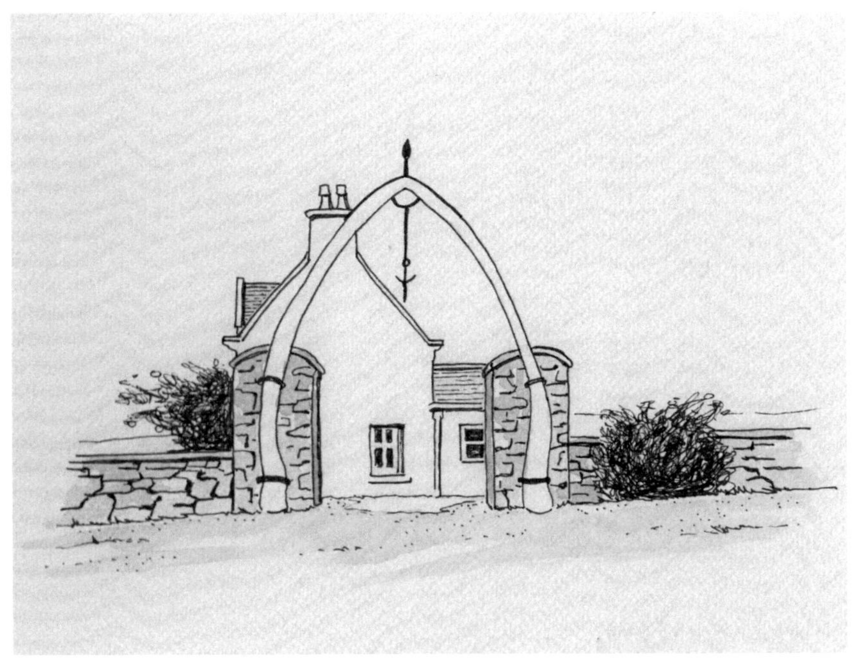

Whalebone Arch, Bragar. The jawbone of an 80 foot blue whale was erected in 1921 to form this unusual arched gateway.

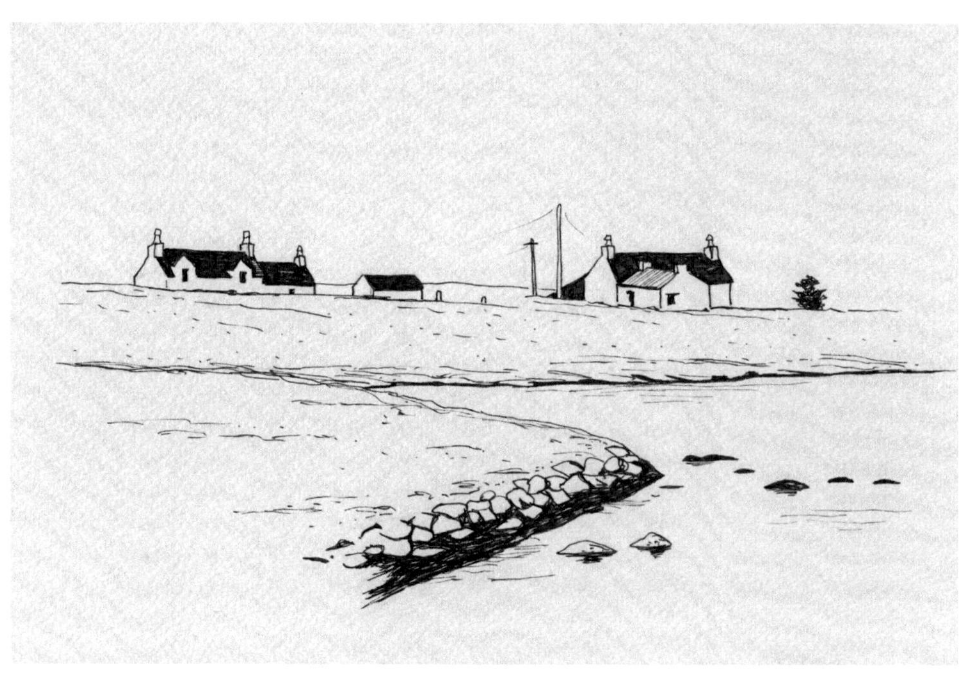

Shawbost crofts.

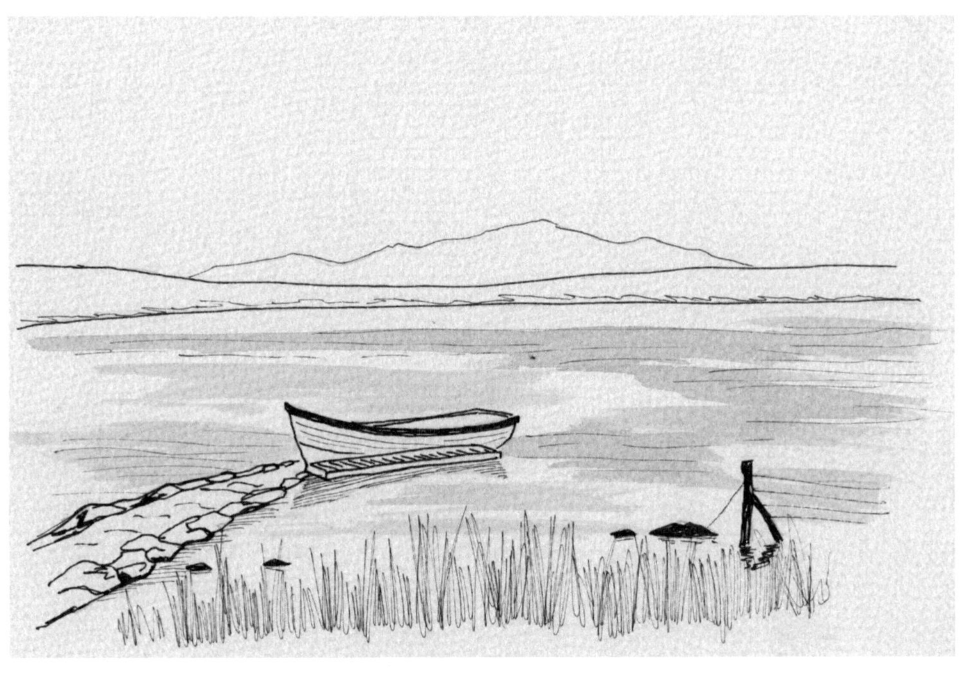

Loch Shawbost. Whilst the sea is ever present, there are also numerous freshwater lochs like this throughout Lewis and Harris.

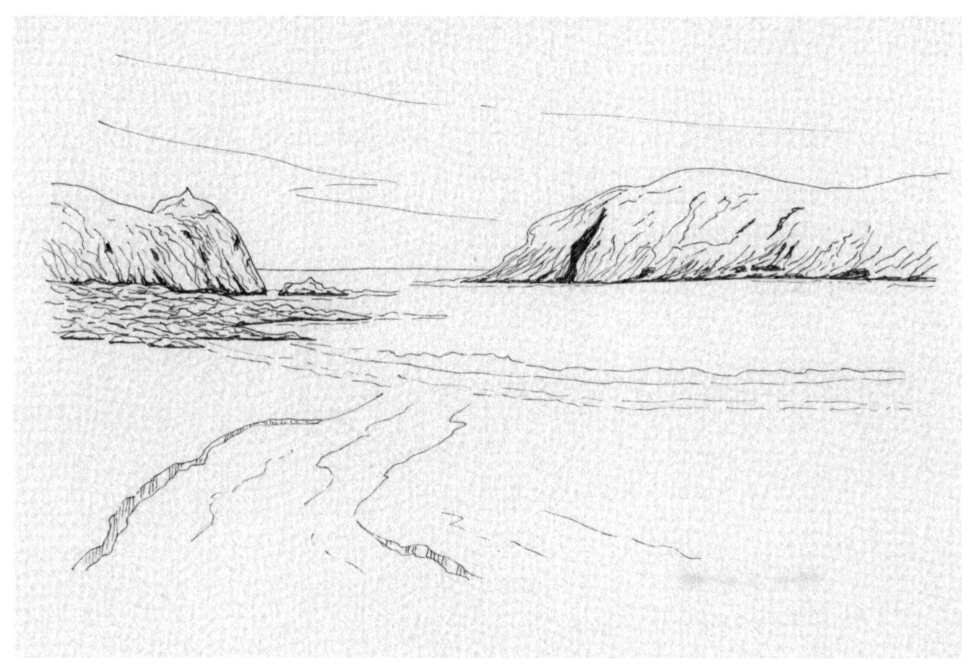

Dalbeg, one of the hidden beaches on the west coast, tucked away at the end of a single track road.

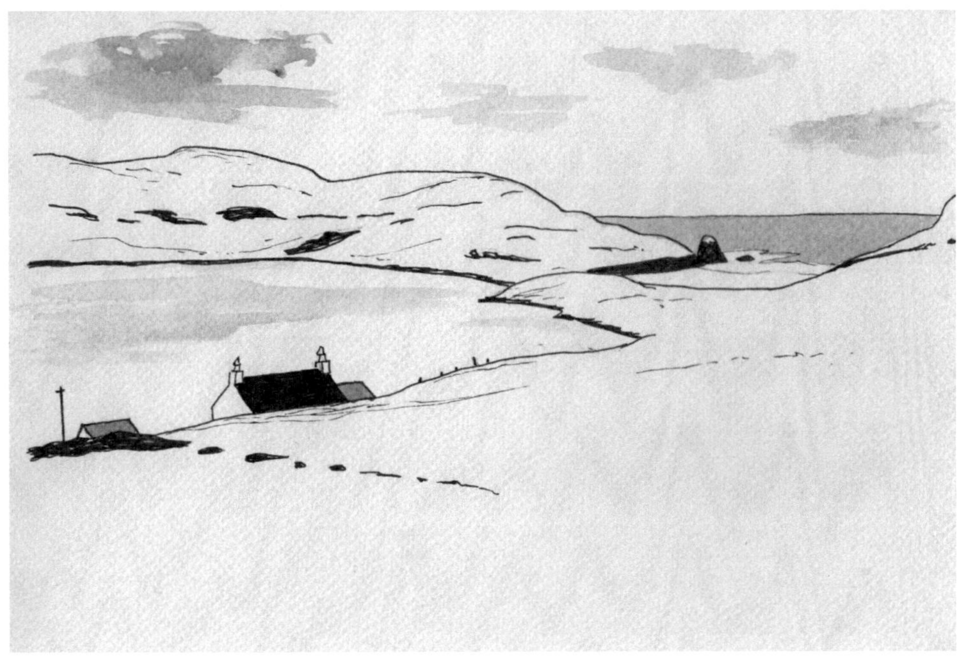

Loch Dalbeg, a freshwater loch which feeds a small stream that runs on to the beach. In summer, the loch is covered with water lilies.

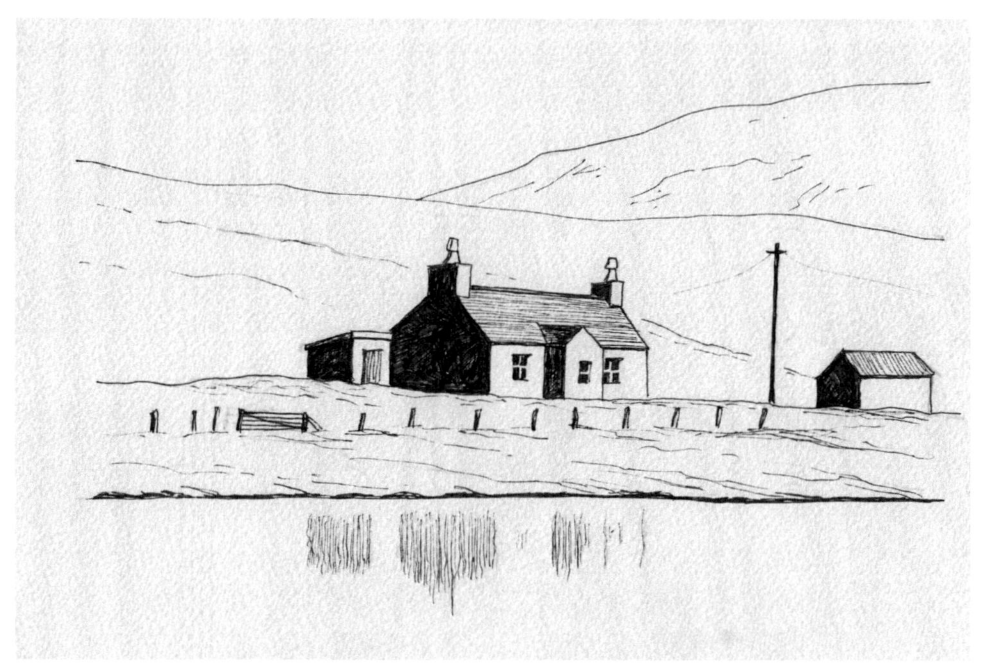

A croft at Dalbeg, between Carloway and Shawbost.

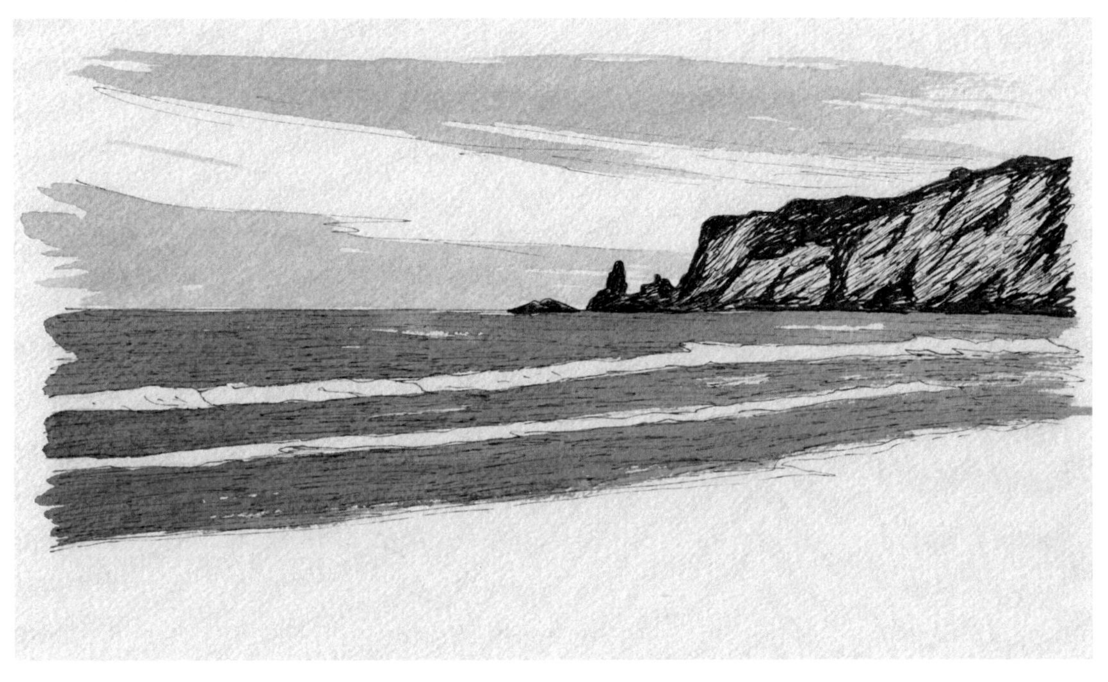

The beach at Dalmore, a destination for surfers.

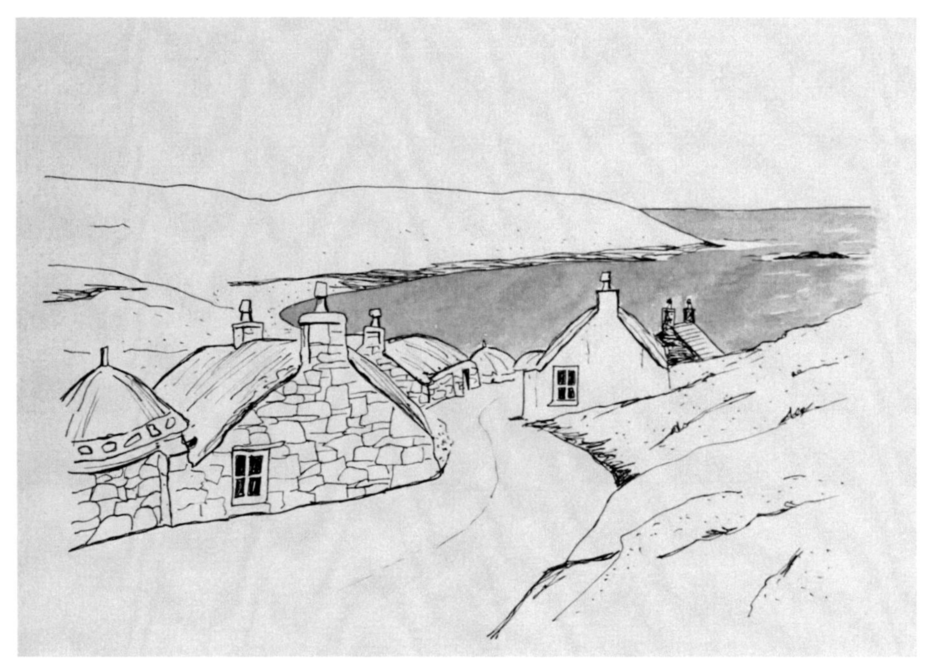

Restored traditional stone thatched cottages at Garenin blackhouse village.

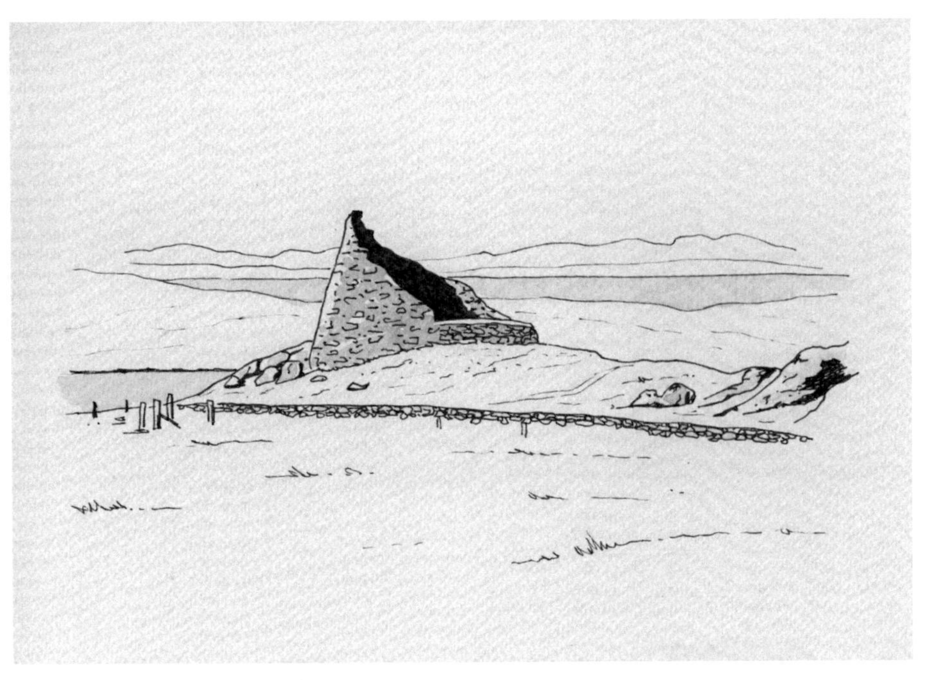

Carloway broch is relatively well preserved; the east wall is 9m high.

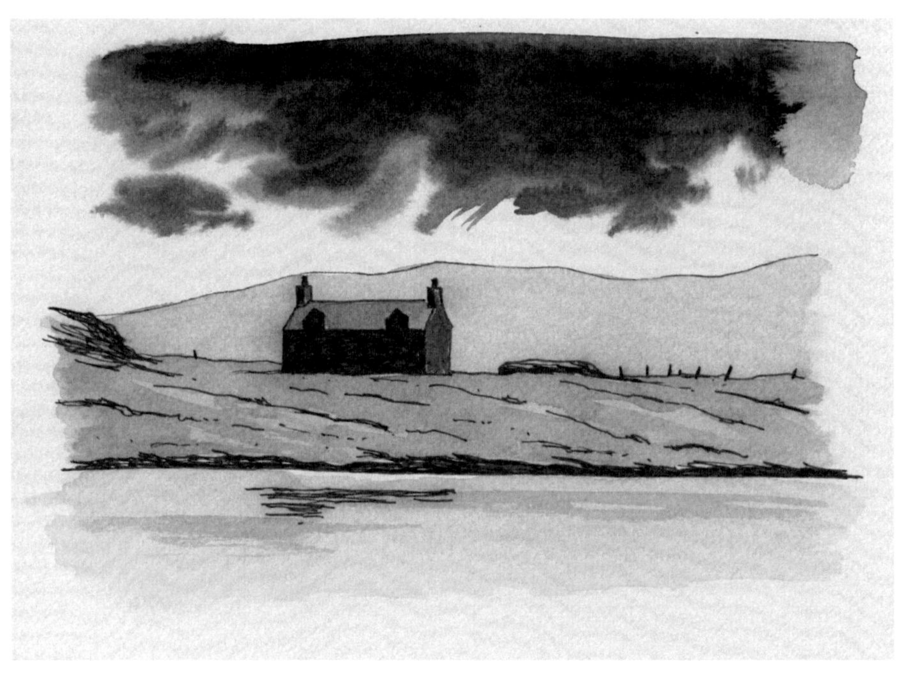

Croft house near Callanish.

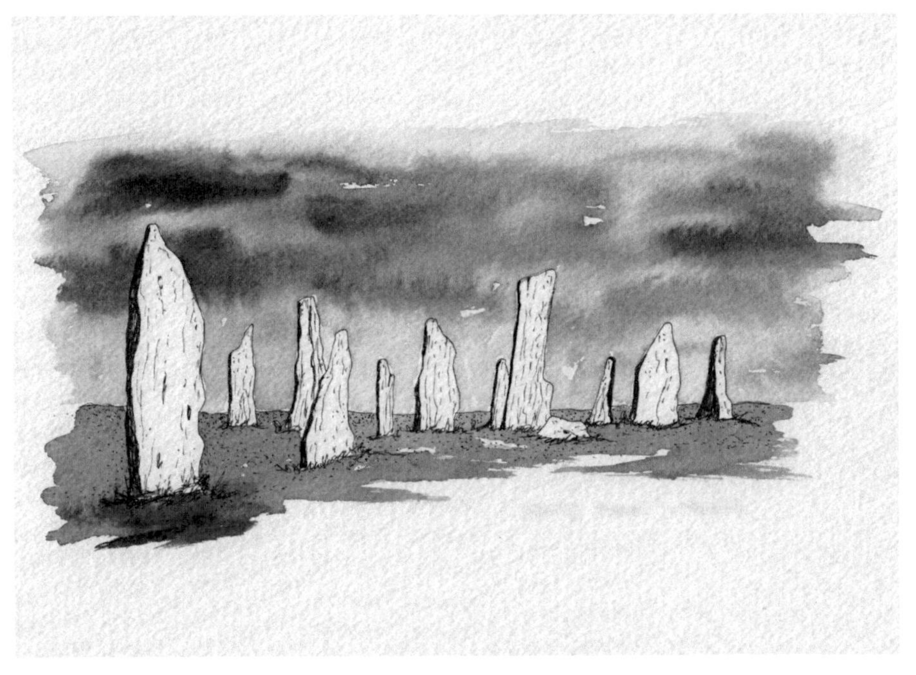

Callanish Standing Stones, drawn one cold February day, not a single person there except me.
This is how I best like to experience the stones.

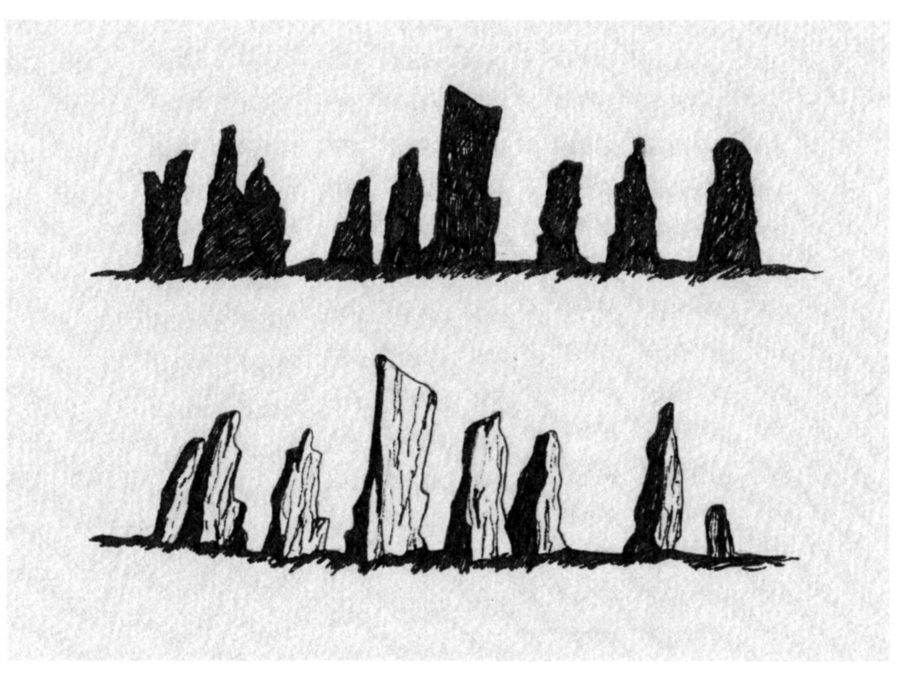

Callanish stones, dating from the late Neolithic era.

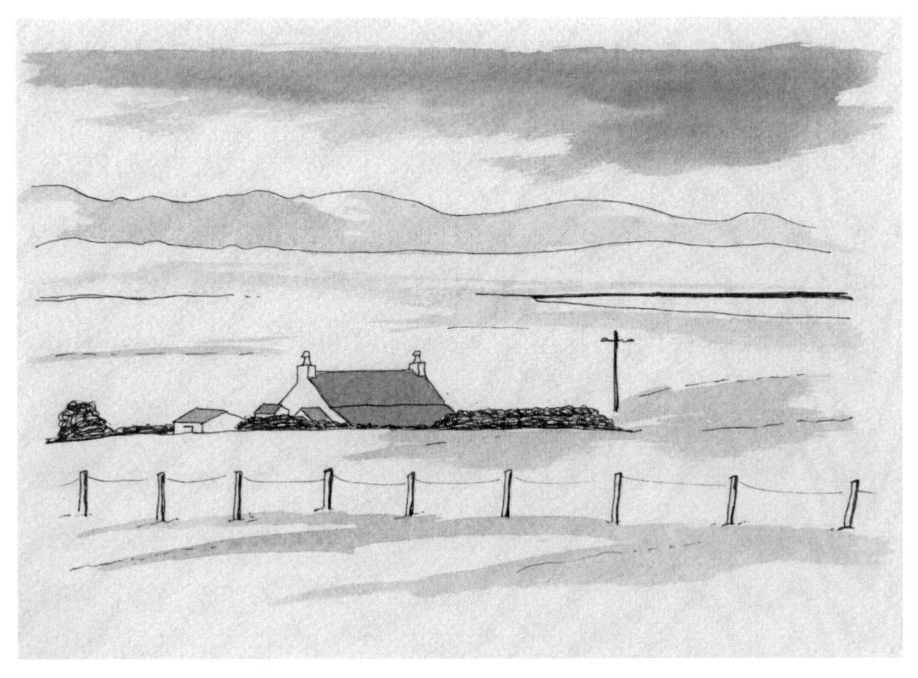

The Harris hills, seen from Achmore.

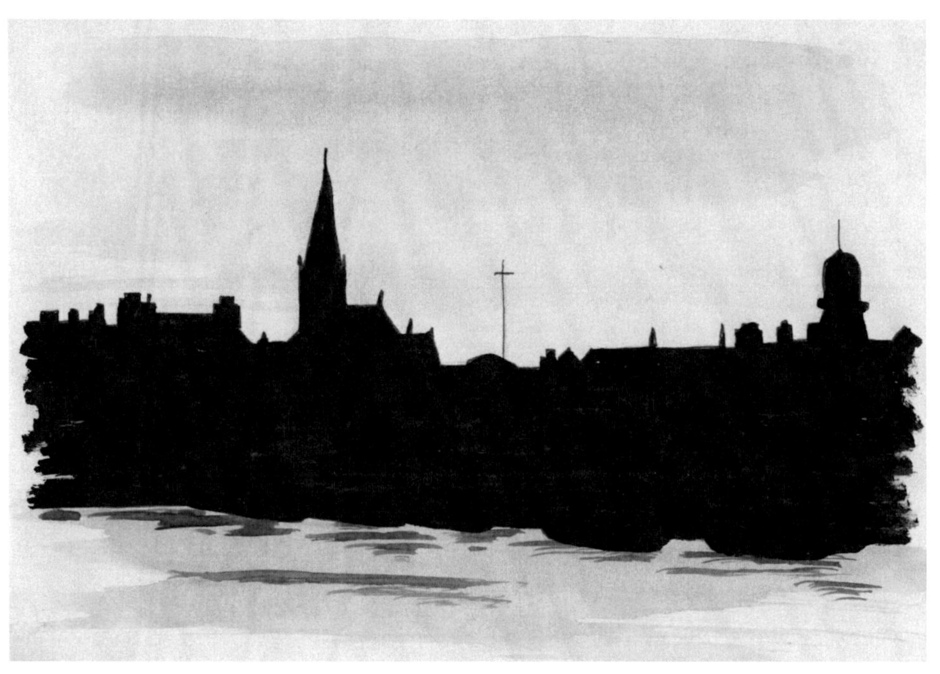

Stornoway, the main port and administrative centre of the Outer Hebrides.

Stornoway and Point Peninsula

STORNOWAY IS THE LARGEST settlement on the island with a population of over 8,000. The town is also the administrative capital for the whole of the Outer Hebrides and the main transport hub. Positioned on a sheltered harbour, Stornoway is the main port with daily passenger and freight ferries to the mainland and home to a small fishing fleet.

The busy harbour, large Victorian buildings, tightly packed houses and shops give the town a busy character which is in sharp contrast to the rest of the island.

To the east of the town is the Point Peninsula which is connected to the rest of Lewis by a thin strip of land known as the Braighe. The peninsula is one of the few areas on the island where the population is increasing.

Diary entry: A wet and windy few days. Local news is reporting that the Braighe Road is closed due to the weather. High seas have thrown boulders and pebbles onto the road and until it is open again, Point will be cut off from the rest of Lewis – and is effectively an island.

Diary entry: It is HebCelt weekend (the annual Hebridean Celtic Music Festival) in the Castle grounds, Stornoway. The population of our small metropolis more than doubles at this time and there is a welcome buzz around the place. As well as taking in the festival we also get to see around twenty impressive sailing ships in the outer harbour as they make an overnight stop on the Tall Ships Race heading to Lerwick.

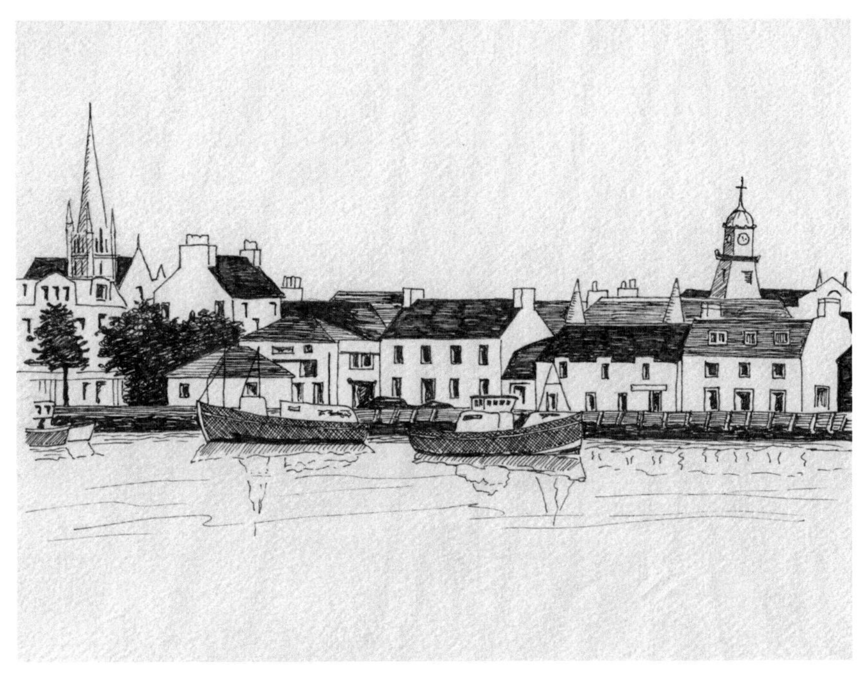

Stornoway harbour.

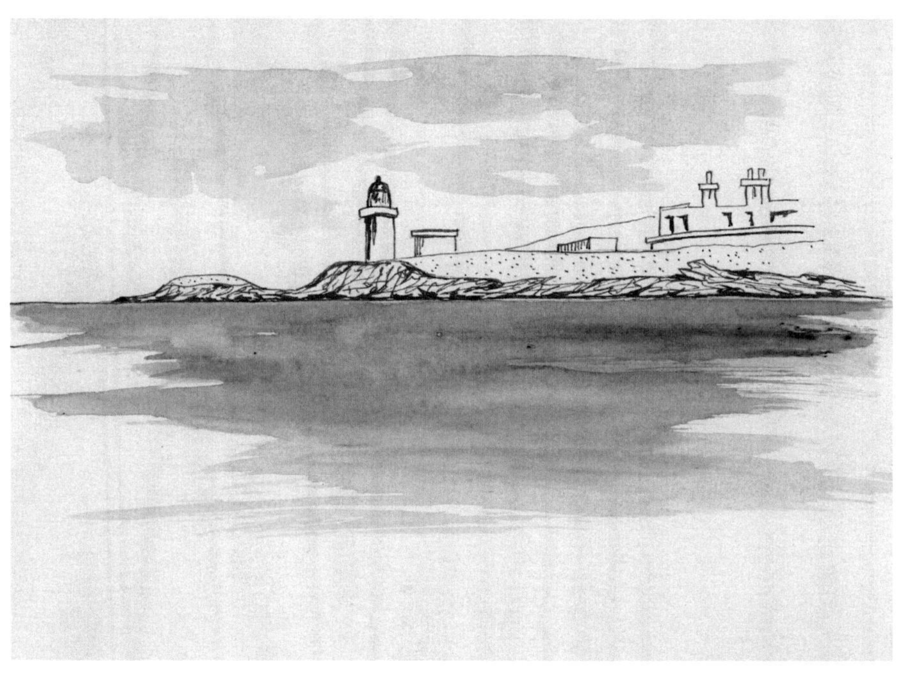

Arnish Point lighthouse marks the entrance to Stornoway outer harbour.

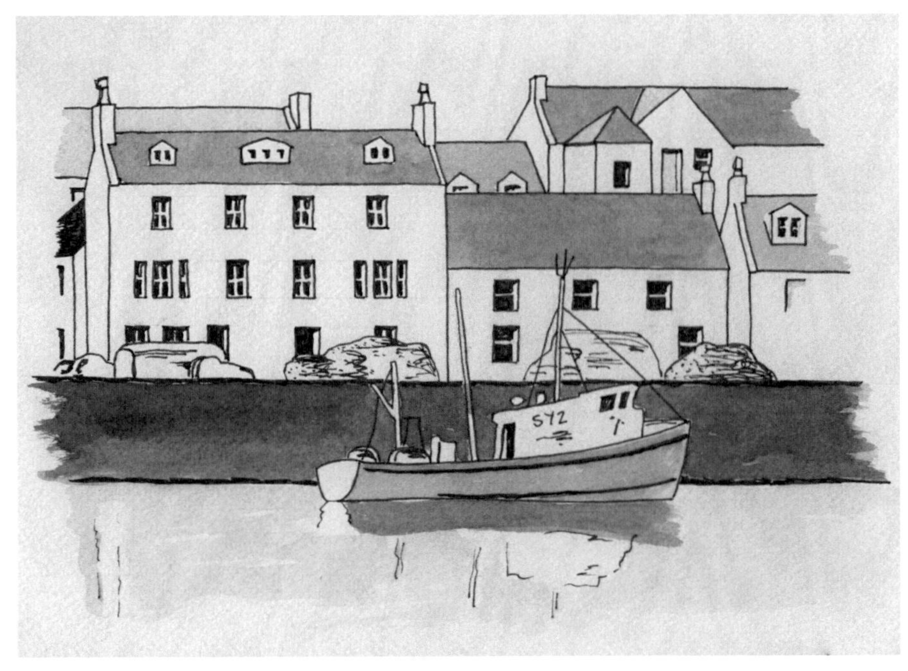

Stornoway inner harbour.

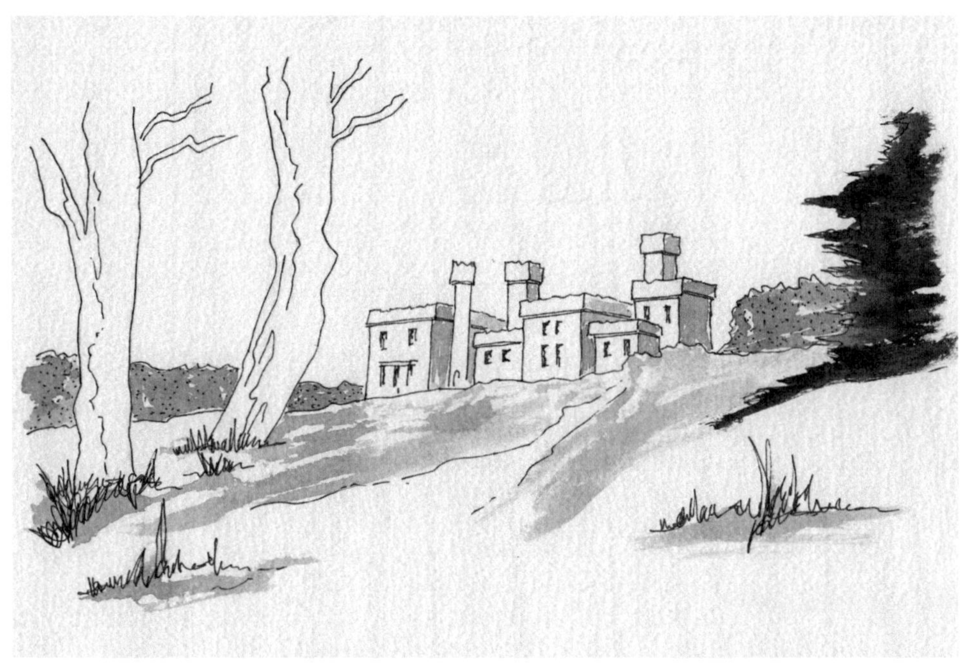

Lews Castle sits in a picturesque position facing the inner harbour. The mock Tudor 'castle' was built by Sir James Matheson in the mid-19th century.

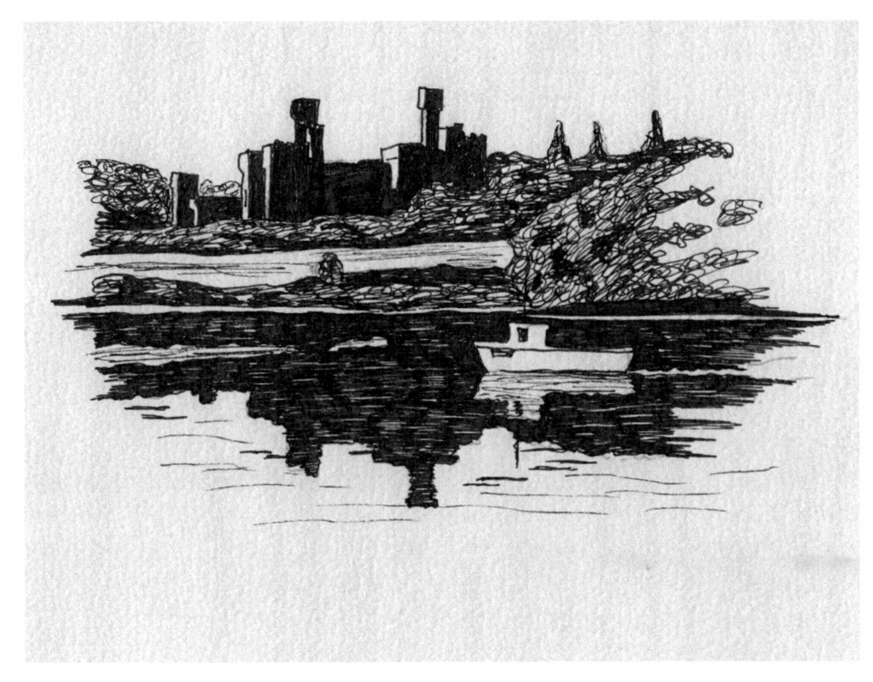

Lews Castle: reflection.

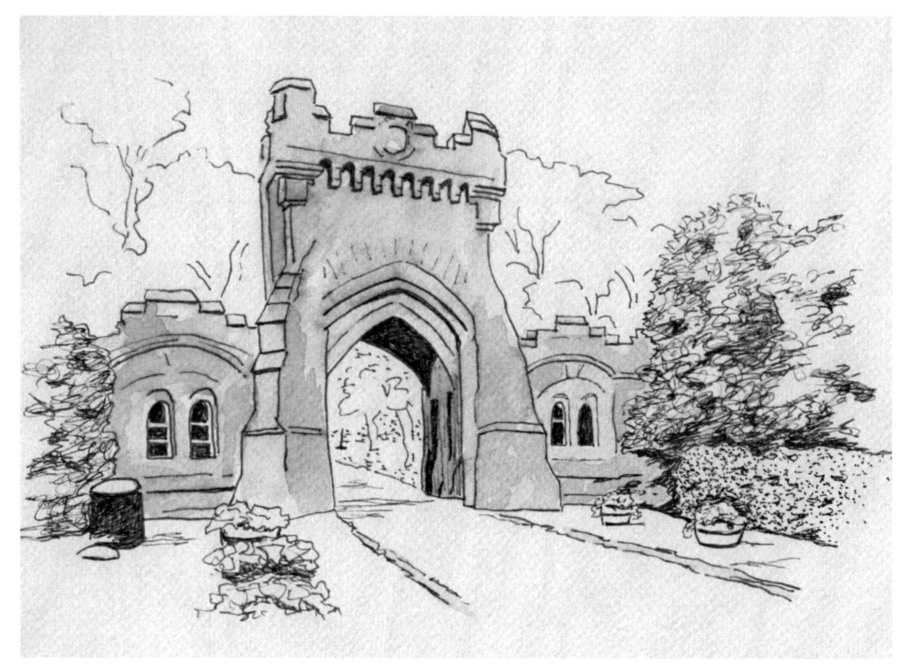

Lews Castle gateway. In 1918 Lord Leverhulme bought Lews Castle from Sir James Matheson. It is now home to the museum of the islands and holiday apartments.

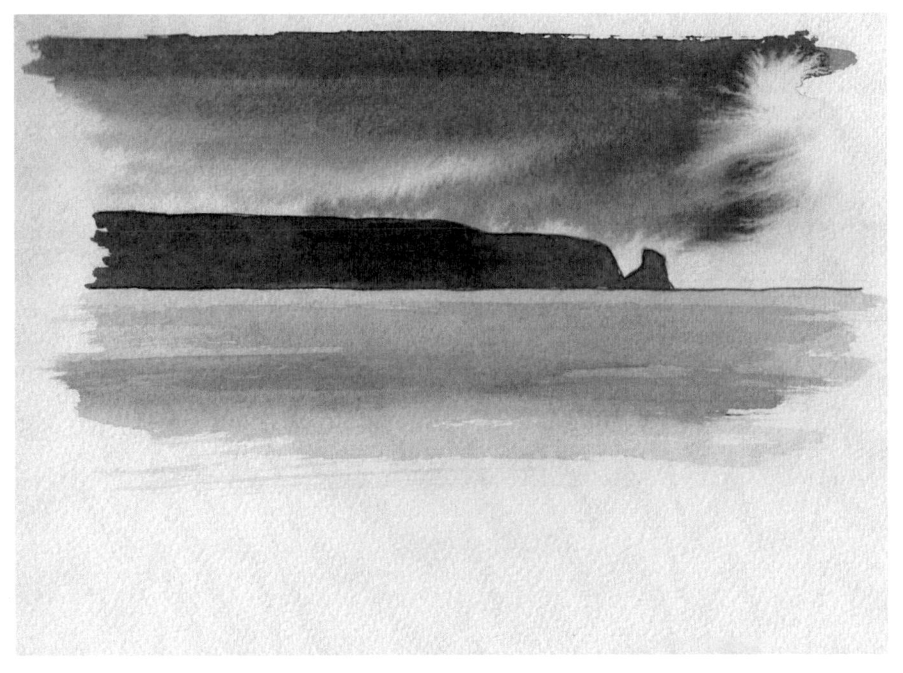

Sea cliffs, Point. Also known as the Eye peninsula, Point is 11km long.

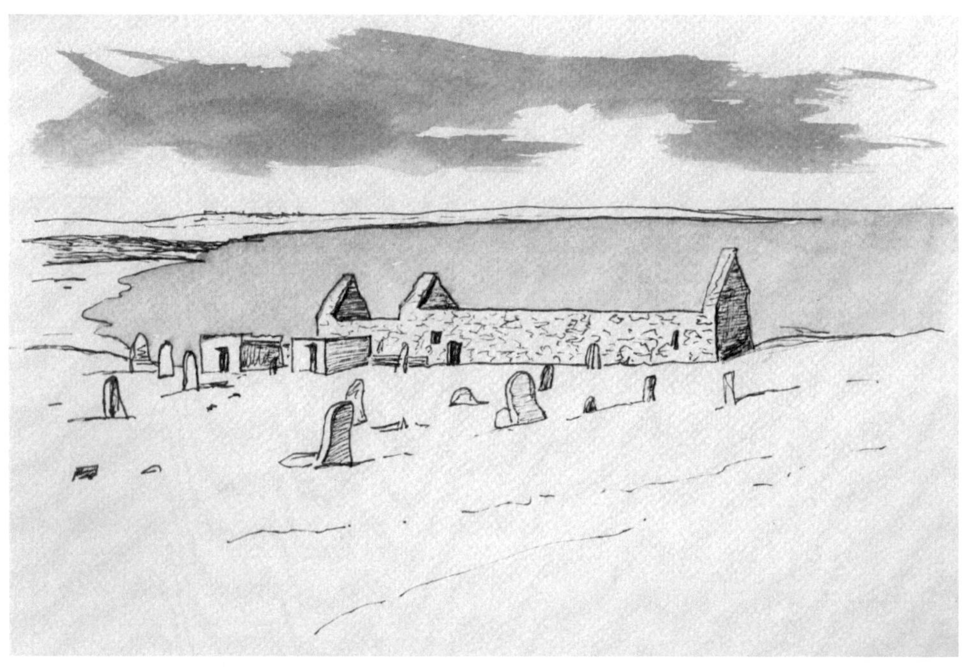

A 14th century church dedicated to Saint Columba at Aignish, now roofless and perilously close to the shore due to coastal erosion.

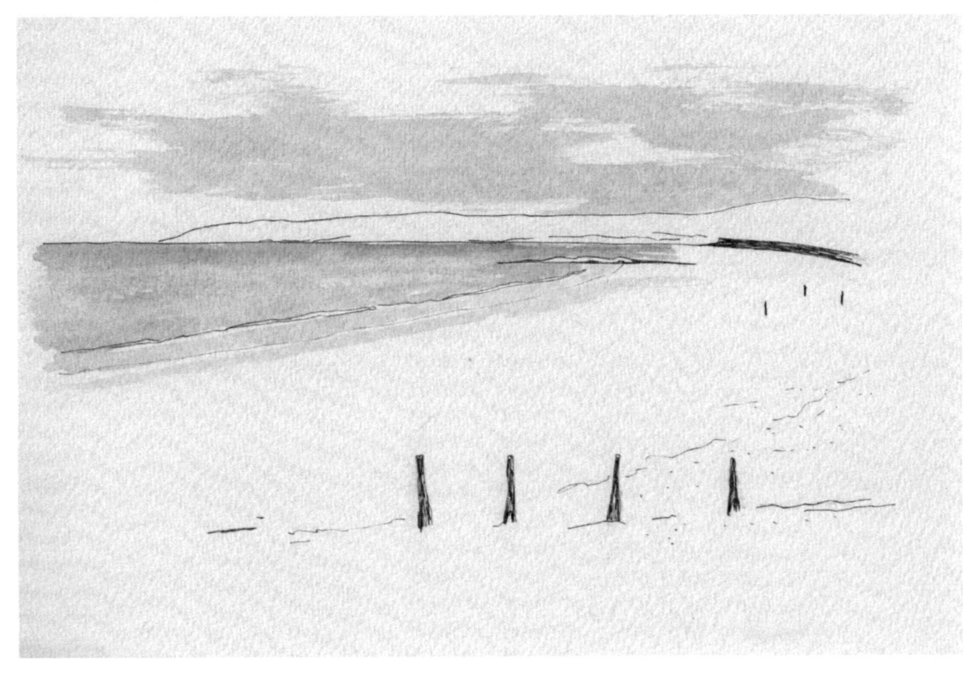

Braighe beach on the narrow isthmus between Stornoway and Point.

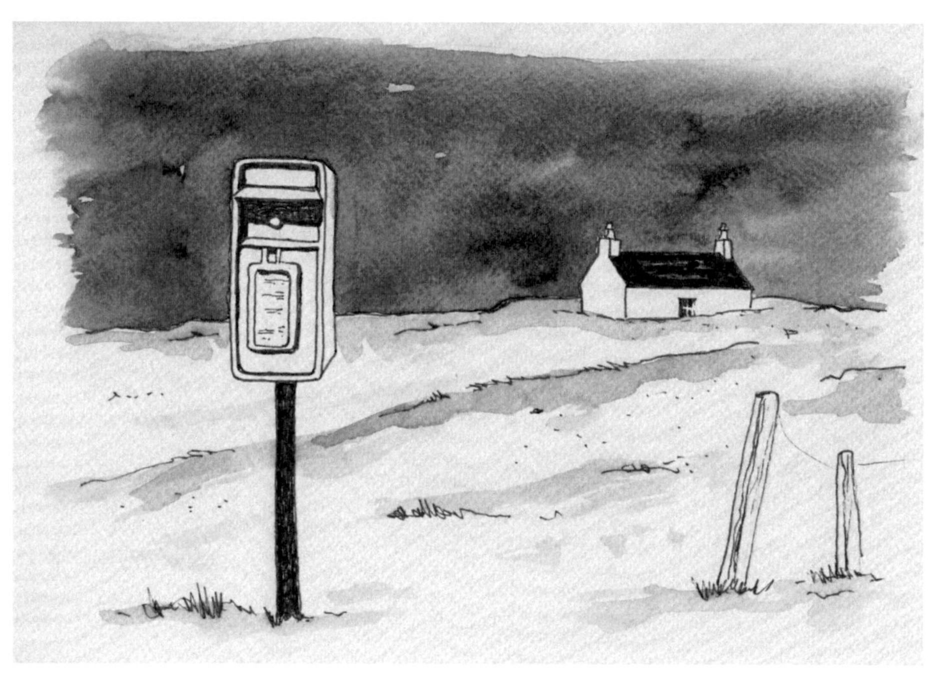

Postbox and croft, Bayble.

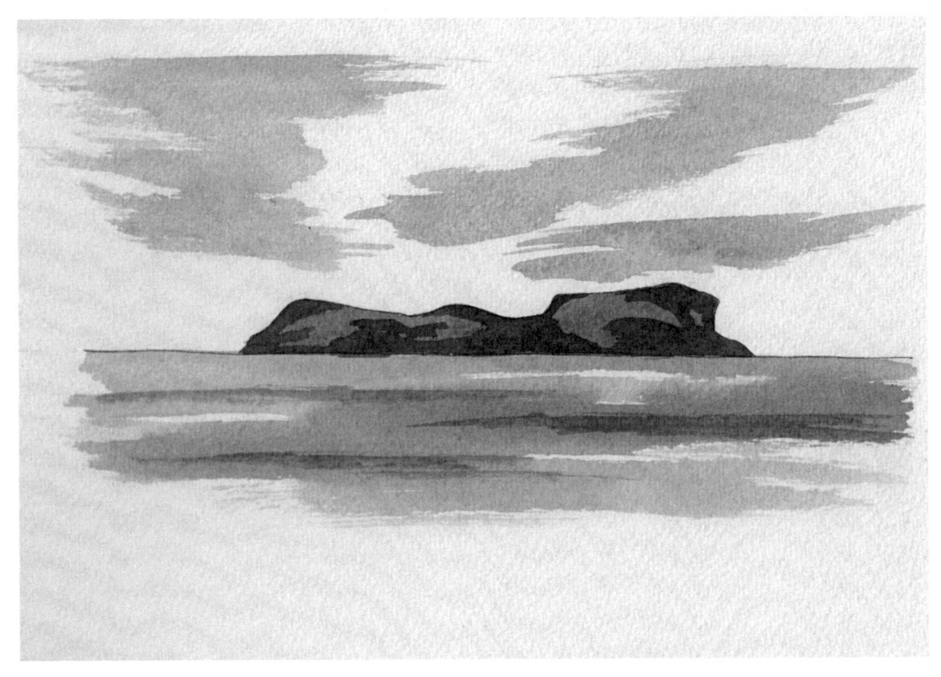

Bayble Island off the south coast of Point is uninhabited.

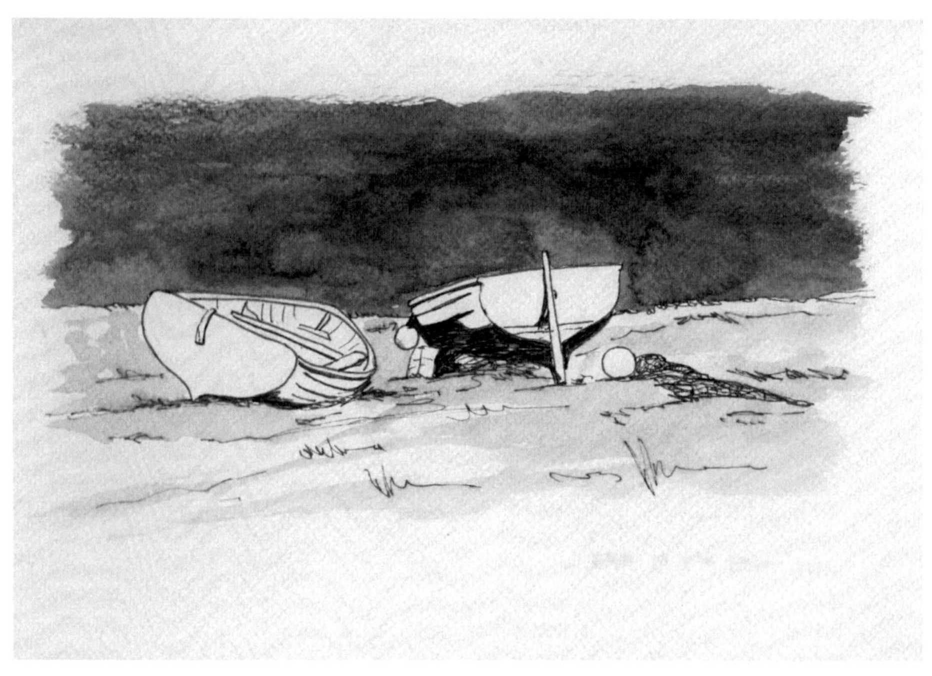

Two boats in a field, Point.

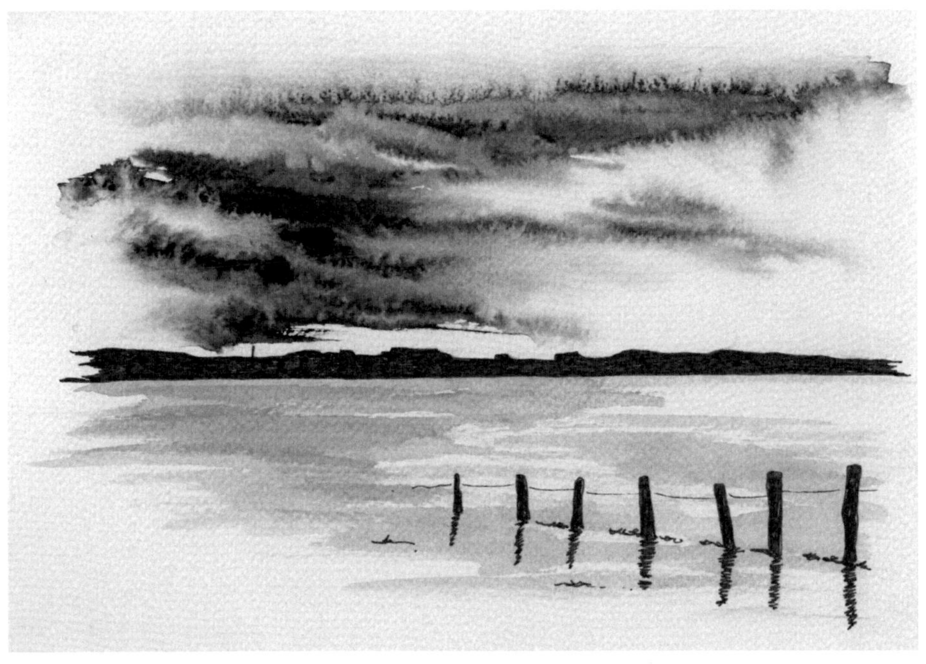

Loch an Tiumpan at the northern end of Point, just before the road ends at Trumpan Head Lighthouse.

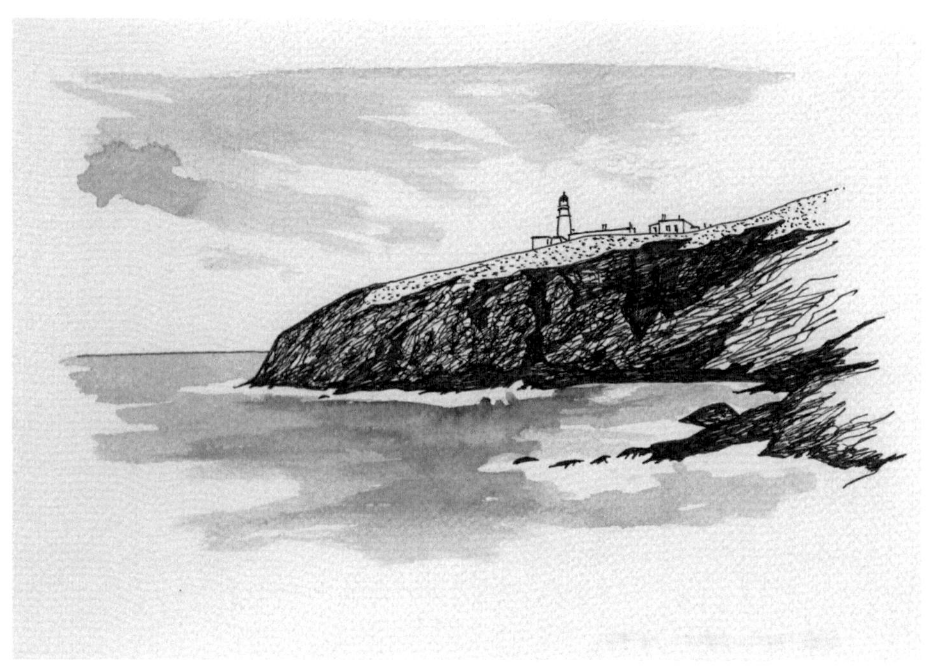

Tiumpan Head Lighthouse, perched on top of the cliffs.

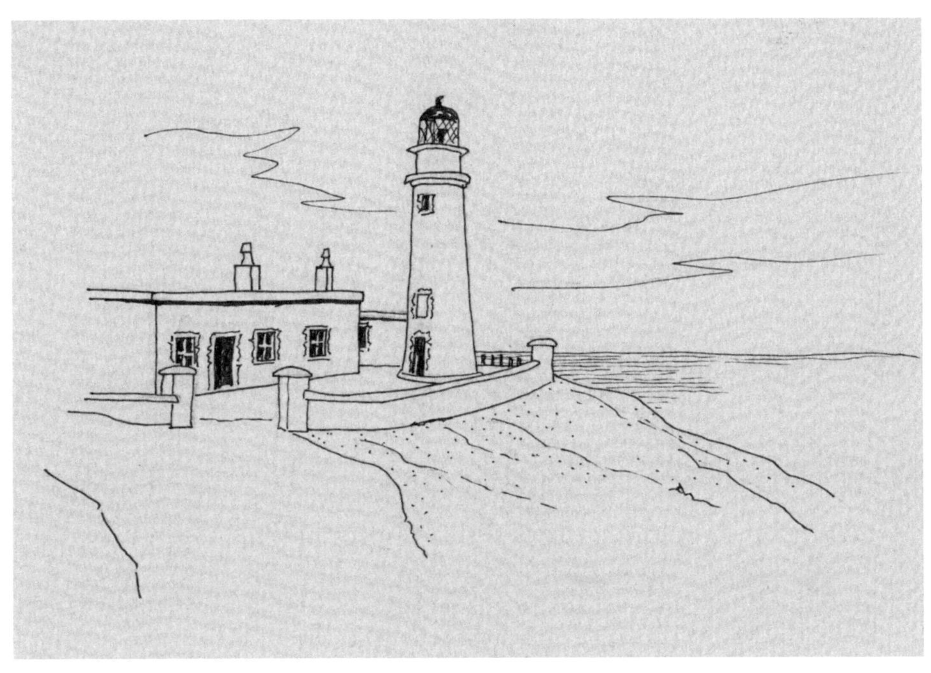

Tiumpan Head Lighthouse, looking across to the mainland hills, now houses kennels and a cattery – the ultimate rooms with a view for pets.

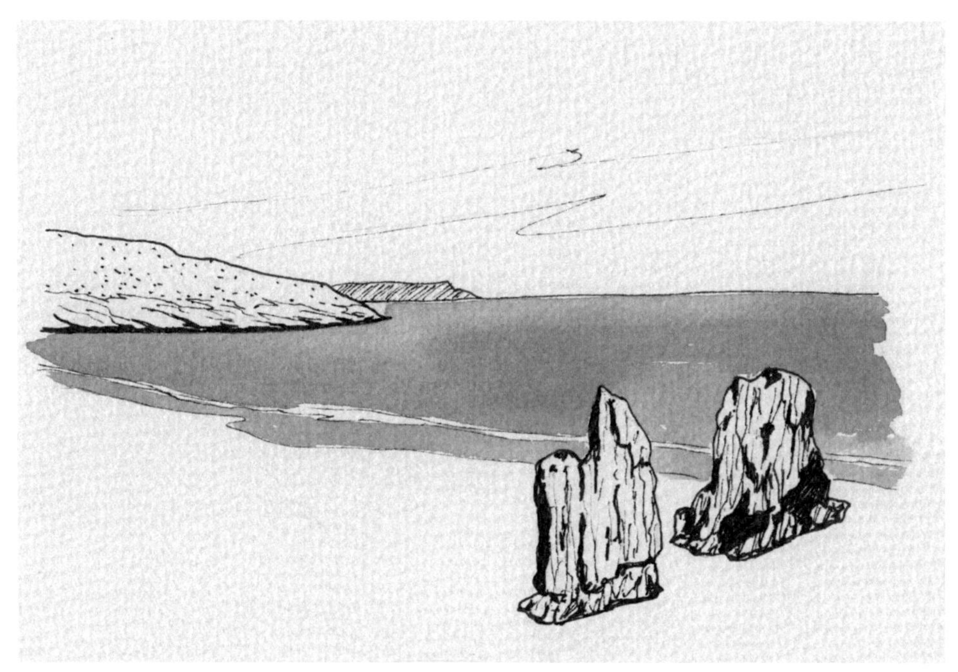

Stacks of Lewisian Gneiss, Garry beach, near the vilage of Tolsta.

Back

THE BACK DISTRICT comprises a number of settlements on the east coast of Lewis, which runs the length of Broad Bay to Tolsta. Between 1919 and 1921 much of the area was the scene of several land raids which resulted in the land being divided into new crofts, many of which still survive today.

There are beaches at Coll, Vatisker and Gress, but Garry beach and the Traigh Mhor at Tolsta are the best known and most popular. The road ends at the car park for Garry beach by the 'Bridge to Nowhere' which was constructed in 1920 by Lord Leverhulme. The intention was to build a road link between Tolsta and Ness, but the road was never completed. The route is now a waymarked footpath across the moorland to Skigersta in Ness.

Crofting is still practised throughout the islands and is the predominant land use in the rural areas.

Diary entry: Looking across to the mainland hills from Tolsta I am reminded of some island humour.

'If you can see the mainland then there is rain on the way. If you can't see the mainland then it is already raining'.

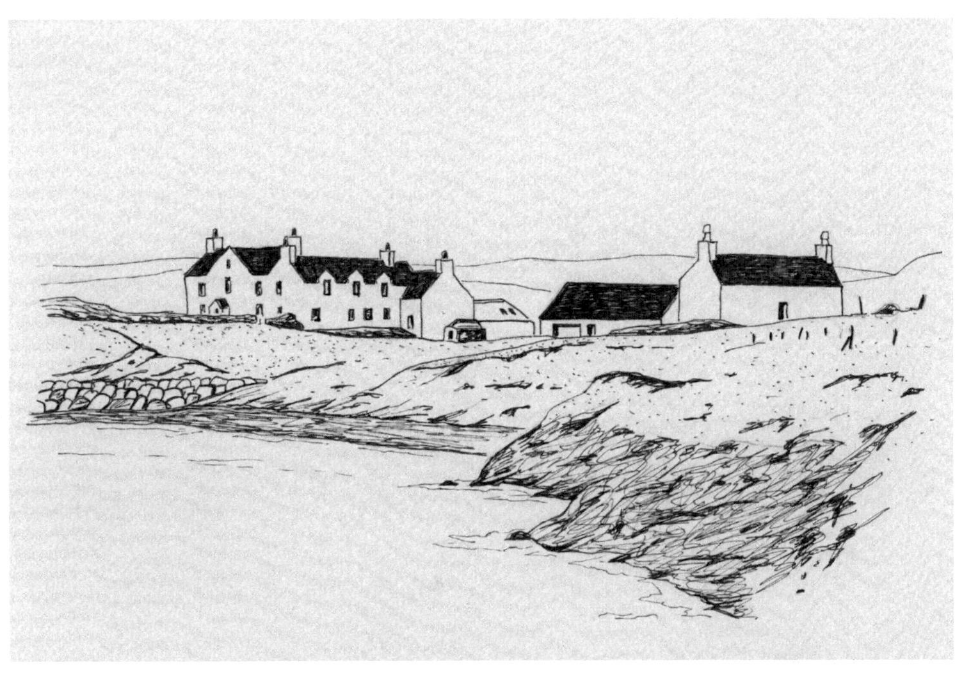

Gress Lodge, a former shooting and fishing lodge overlooking Broad Bay.

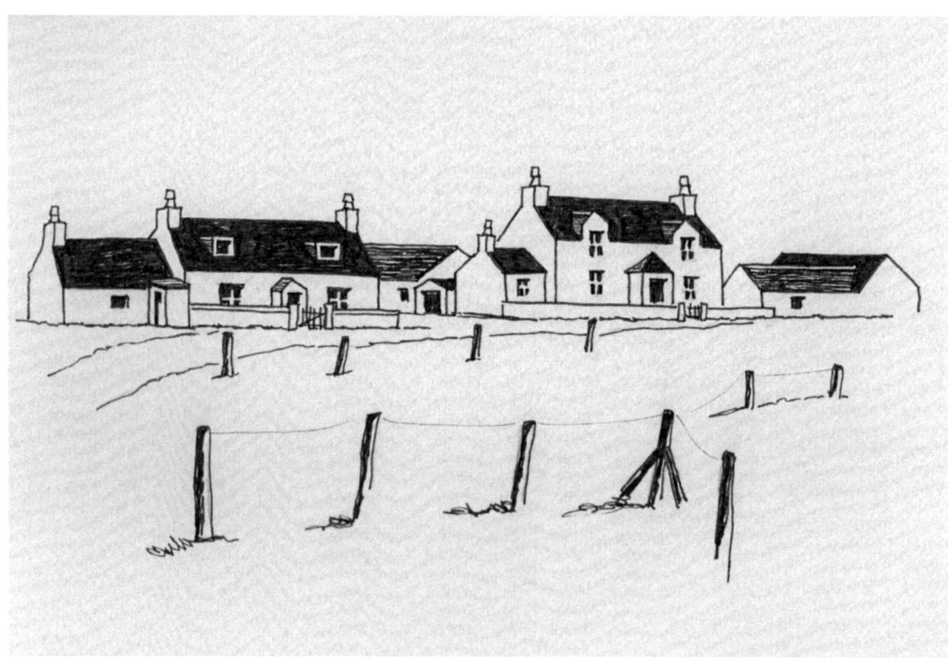

Crofts. Tolsta is made up of three crofting settlements: North Tolsta, Glen Tolsta and New Tolsta.

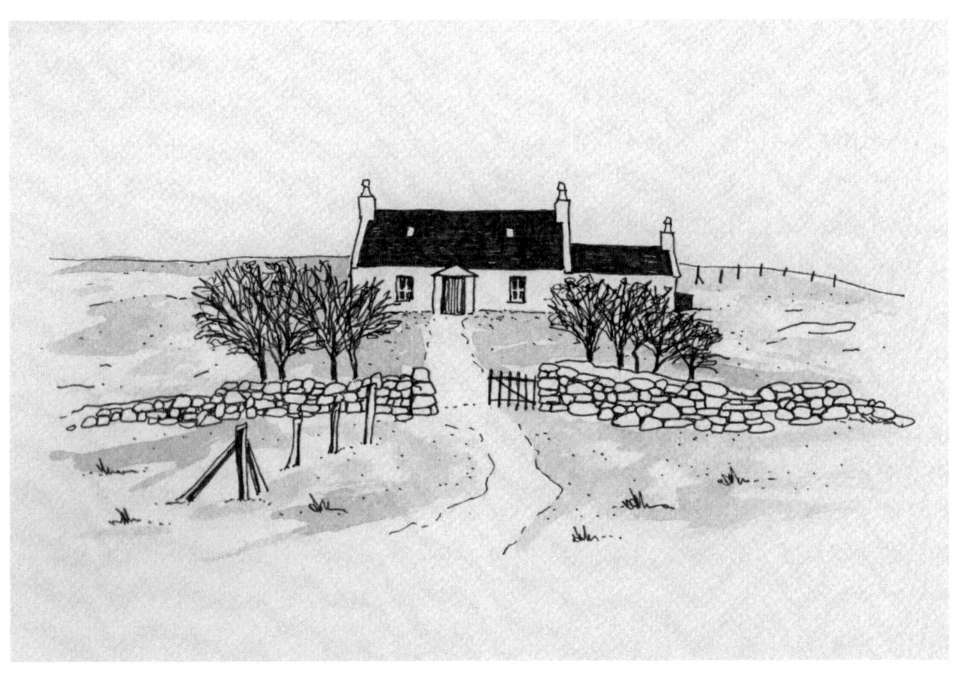

Walled croft, Tolsta.

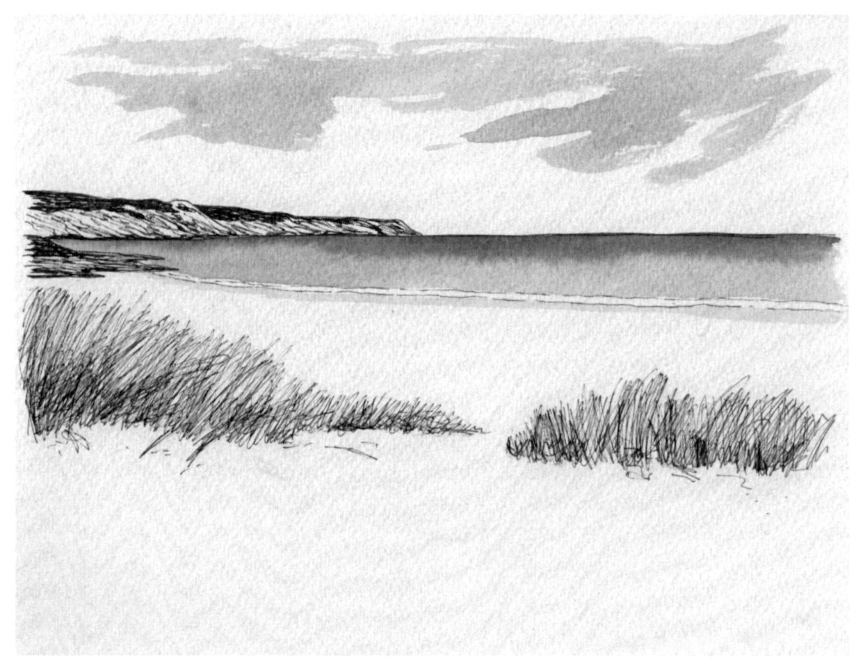

Sand dunes, Tolsta.

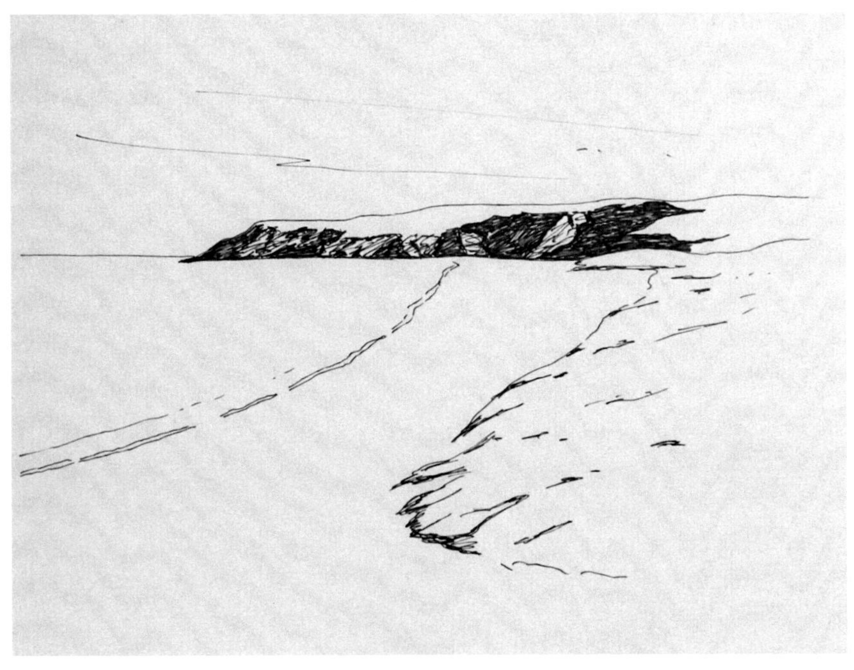

Traigh Mhor, Tolsta. A short, steep descent leads to this long beach backed by sand dunes.

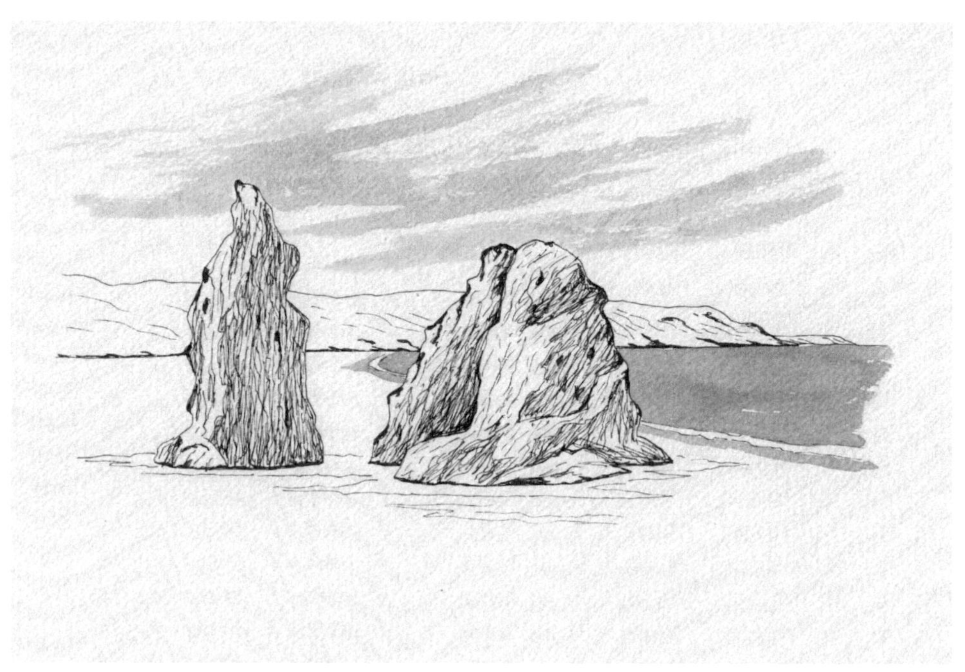

Sea stacks, Garry beach. There are two beaches in Tolsta, Traigh Mhor and Garry beach. The road ends at Garry, where it turns into a car park by the ill-fated 'Bridge to Nowhere'.

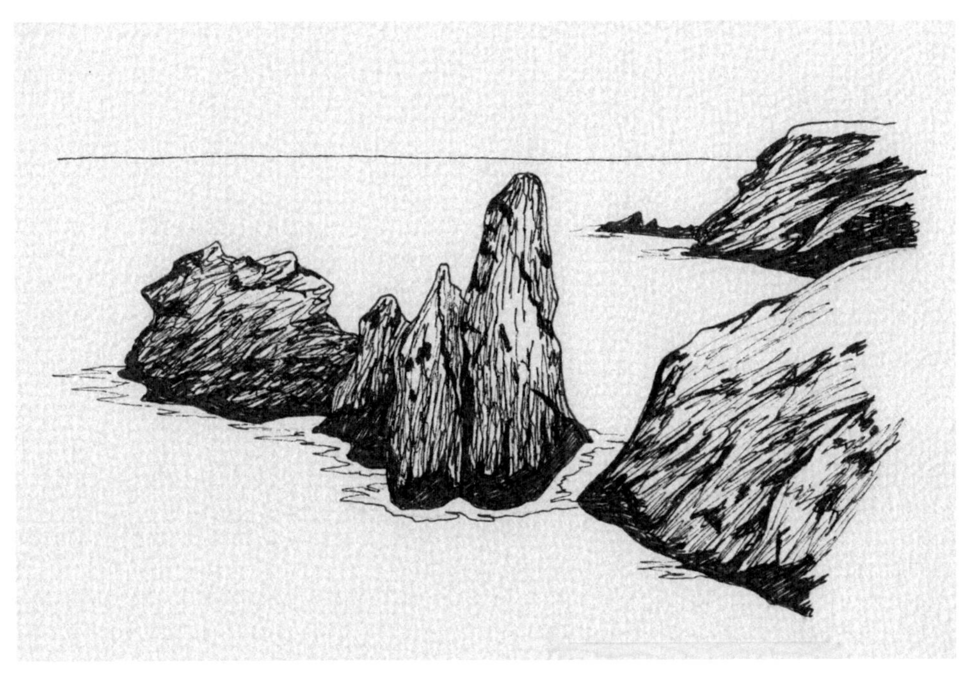

Tolsta Head.

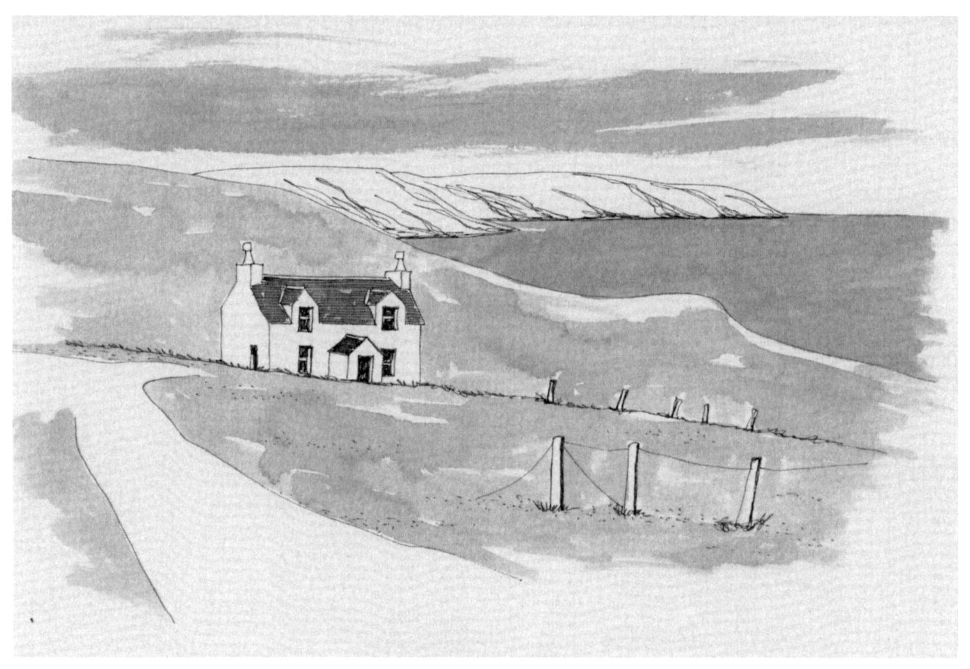

Croft in New Tolsta. A single track road leads north to the sea and the 'Bridge to Nowhere'.

North and South Lochs

THE LOCHS AREA lies to the south of Stornoway in southeast Lewis. As the name suggests, the district has an abundance of both freshwater and saltwater lochs dotted around the rugged landscape. Both North and South Lochs are sparsely populated, with the Park area in the south being the most empty, with a population as low as 400. The remains of villages and settlements abandoned due to the Clearances in the 19th century can still be seen here. A monument by the main road, just south of Balallan, commemorates the Park Deer Raid carried out here in 1887.

Diary entry: An article on the BBC news website about a cull of black rats on the uninhabited Shiant Islands (in the Minch, east of Lewis) tells of how the now native black rats are seriously affecting the resident breeding seabird colonies. Various figures from £450,000 to £1 million are estimated as the possible cost for the Seabird Recovery Project. Apparently the ancestors of the present day rats were thought to have come ashore from shipwrecks in the 1900s and have been preying on the seabirds ever since.

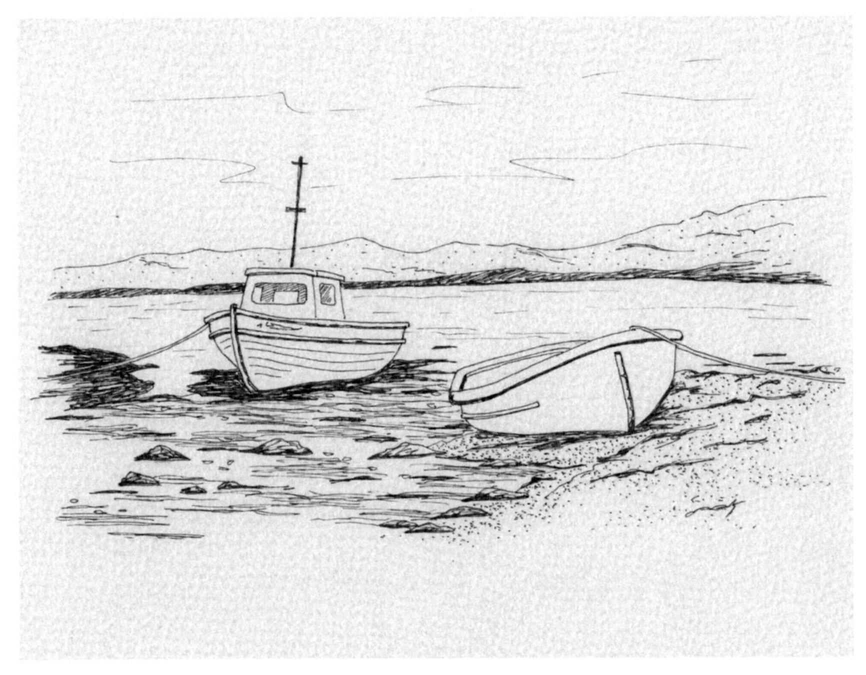

Boats, Ranish.

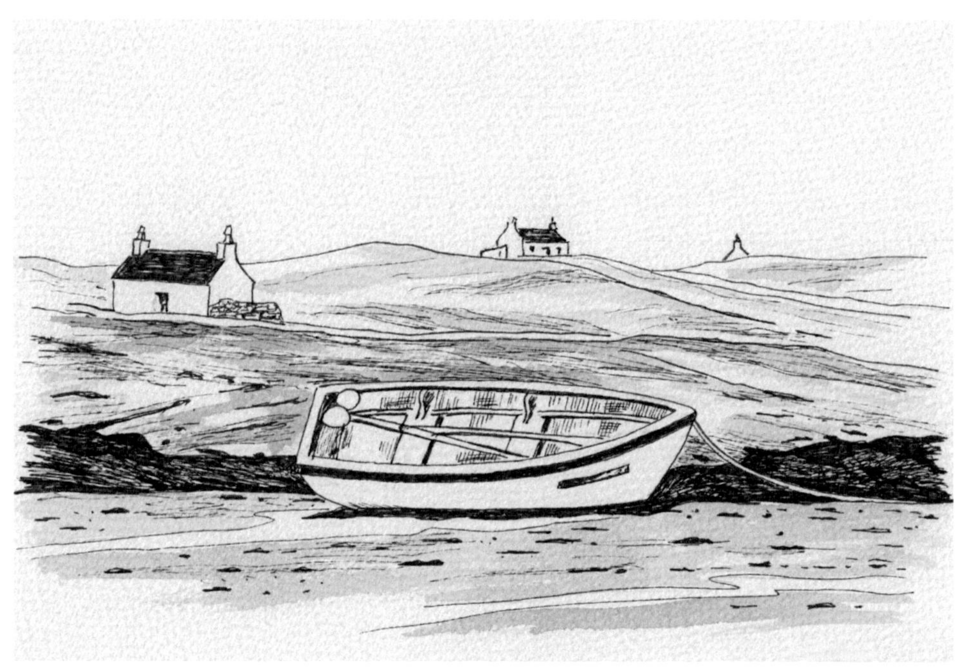

Low tide, Ranish.

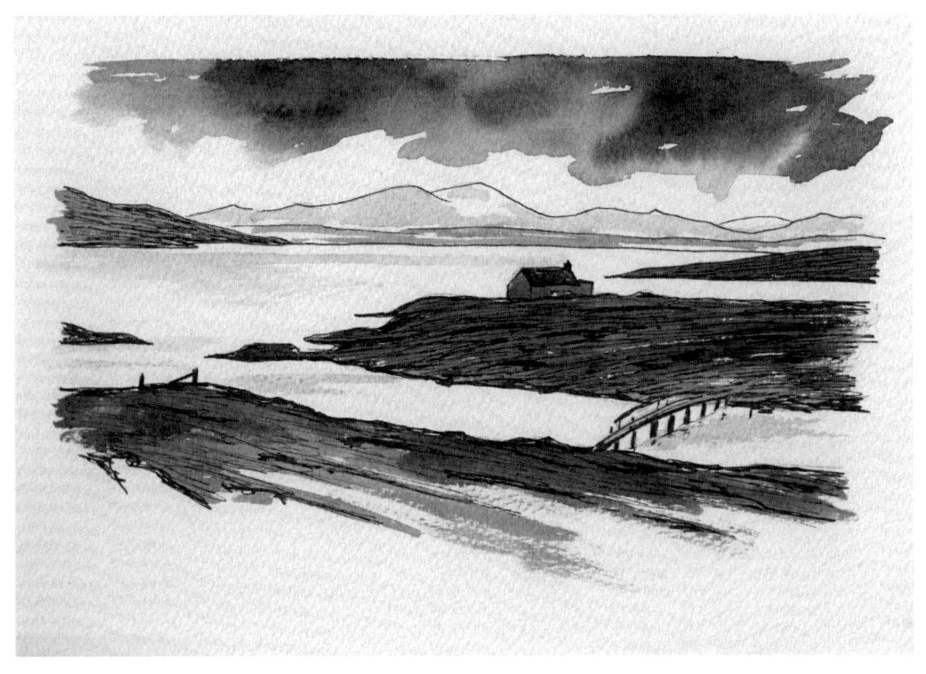

Bothy, Laxay, where the River Laxay runs into Loch Valtos.

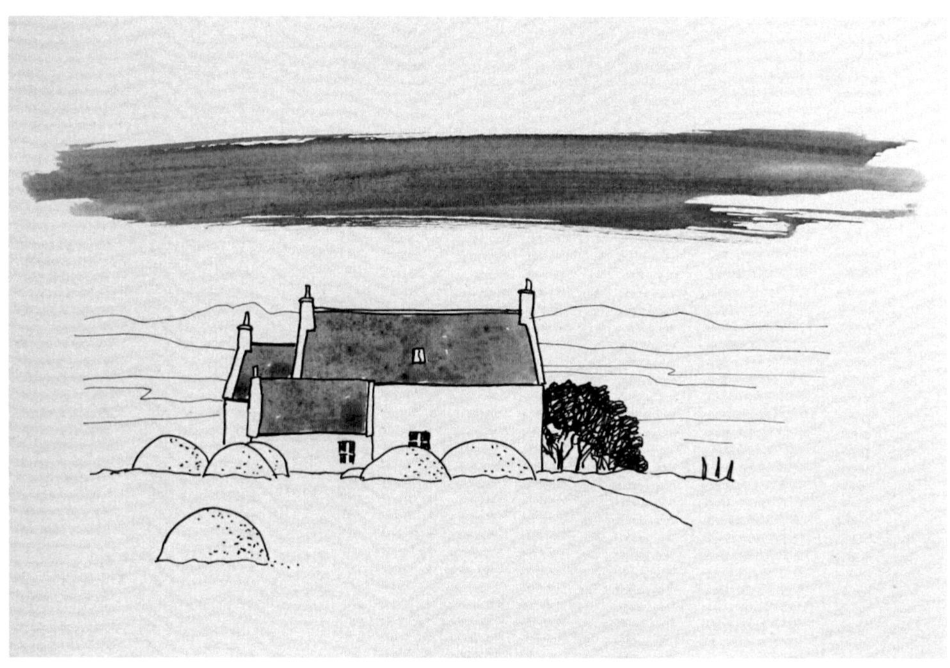

Croft and haystacks, Balallan. Four miles from end to end, this settlement is the longest in Lewis.

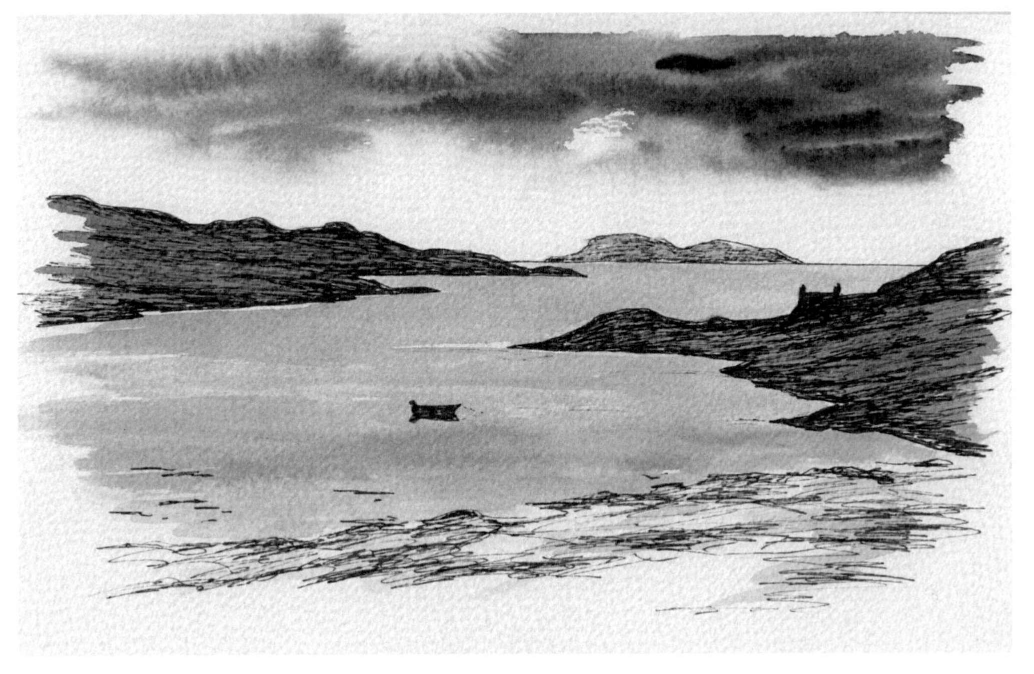

Shiant Islands.

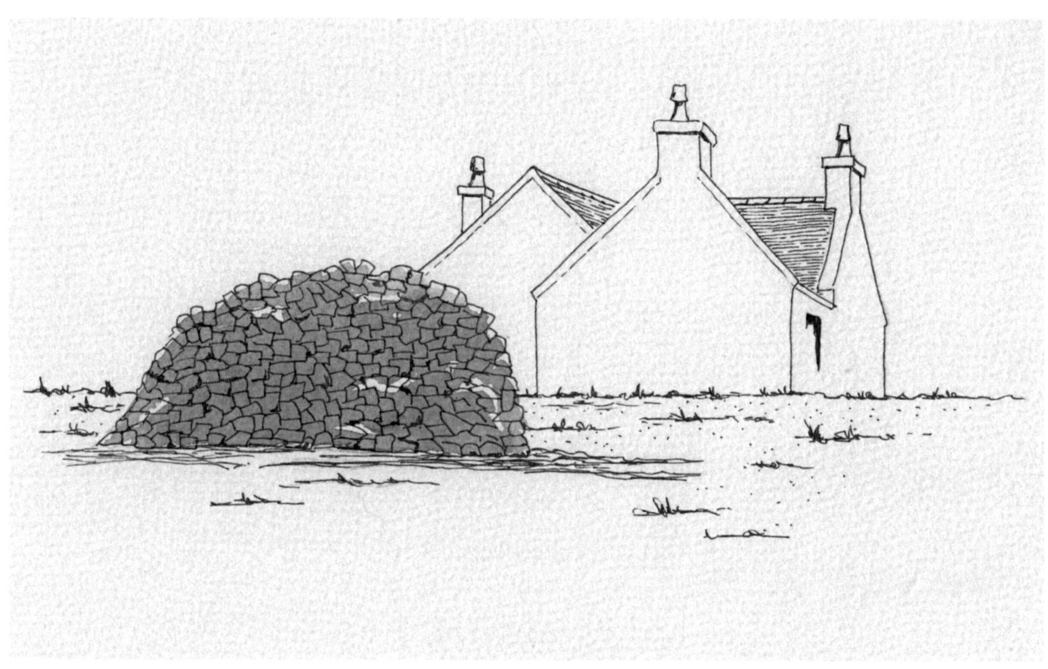

Croft and peatstack, Balallan. Crofting has changed little over the years and the traditional small scale, low impact farming is in evidence throughout the seasons.

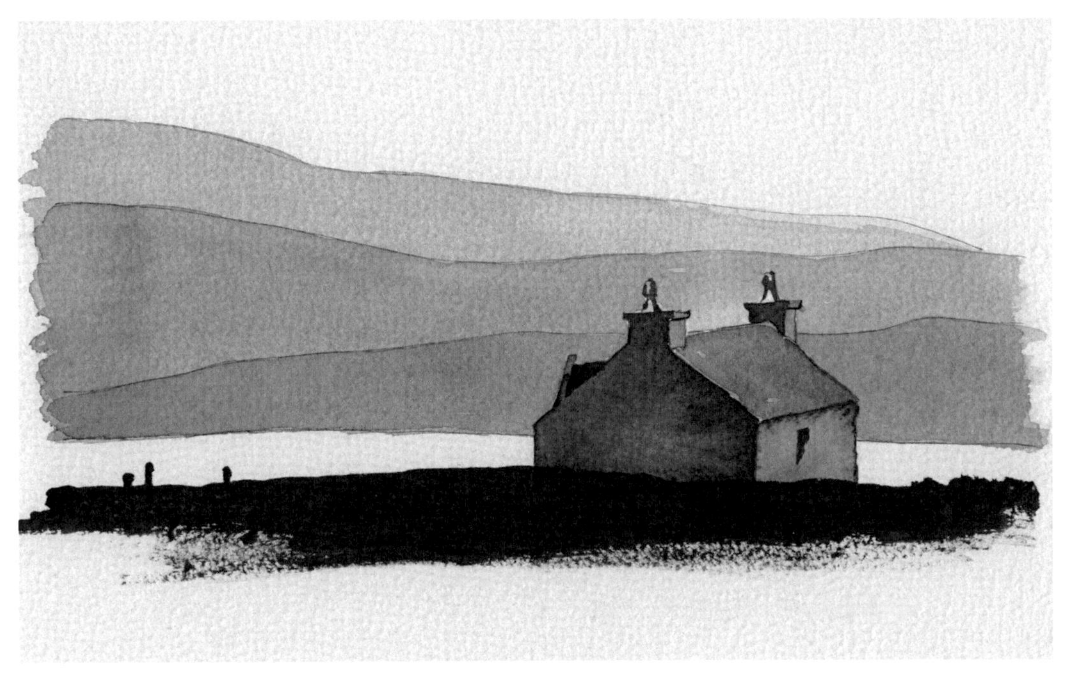

Hills above Loch Erisort.

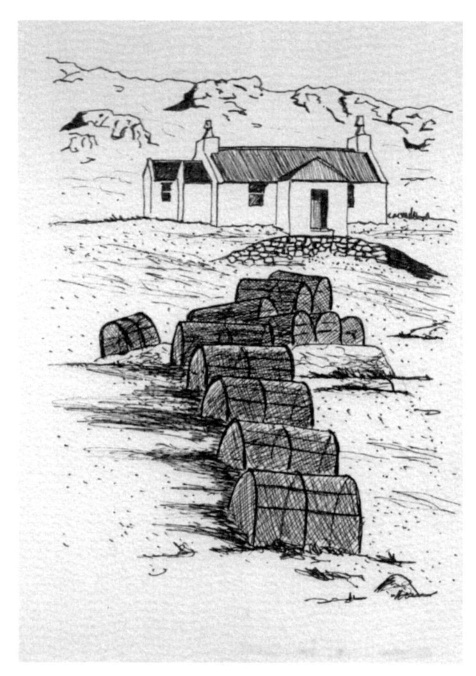

Fisherman's bothy, Crossbost.

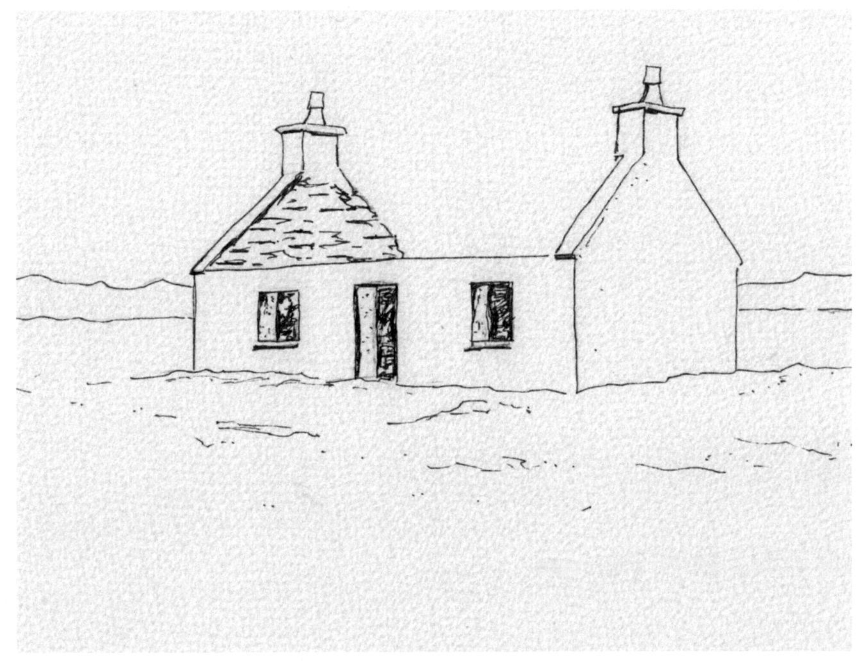

Abandoned croft, Park. Much of South Lochs is a wilderness and a sad legacy of the Clearances.

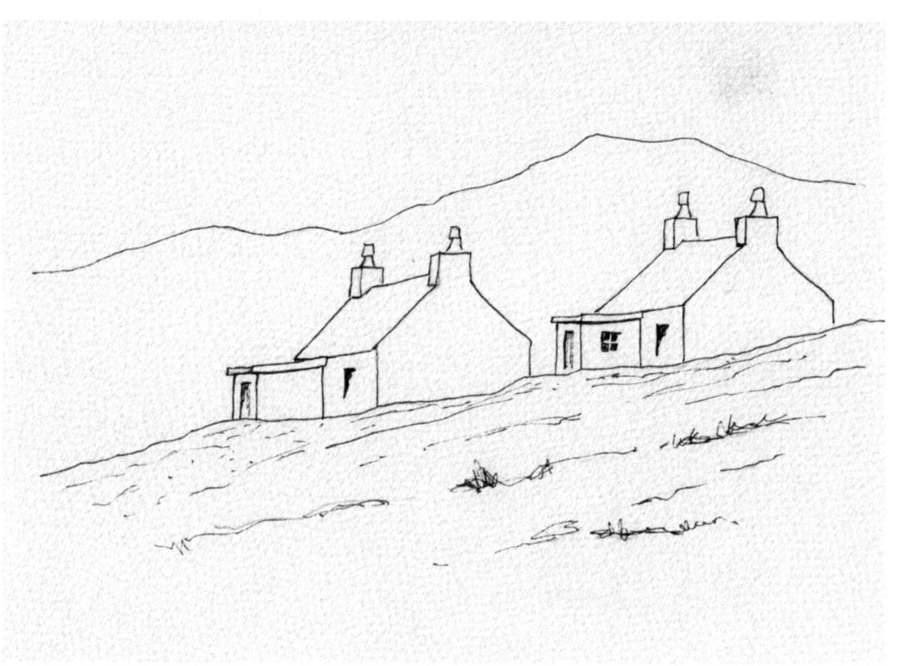

Crofts at Lemreway.

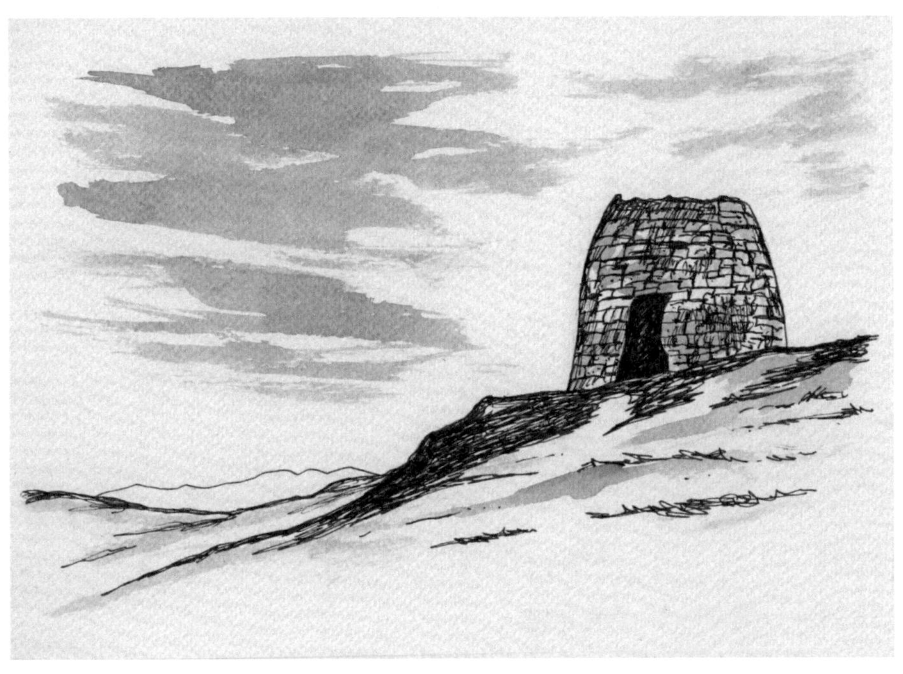

A large cairn designed by Will Maclean, commemorating the Deer Raids of 1887, occupies a prominent position on the Stornoway to Tarbert road.

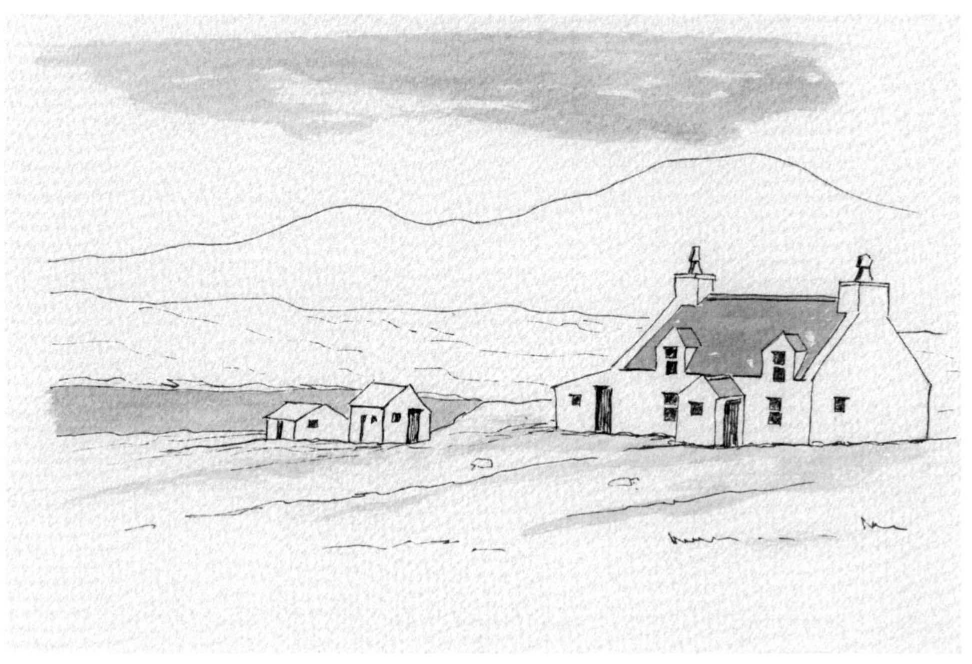

Arivruach.

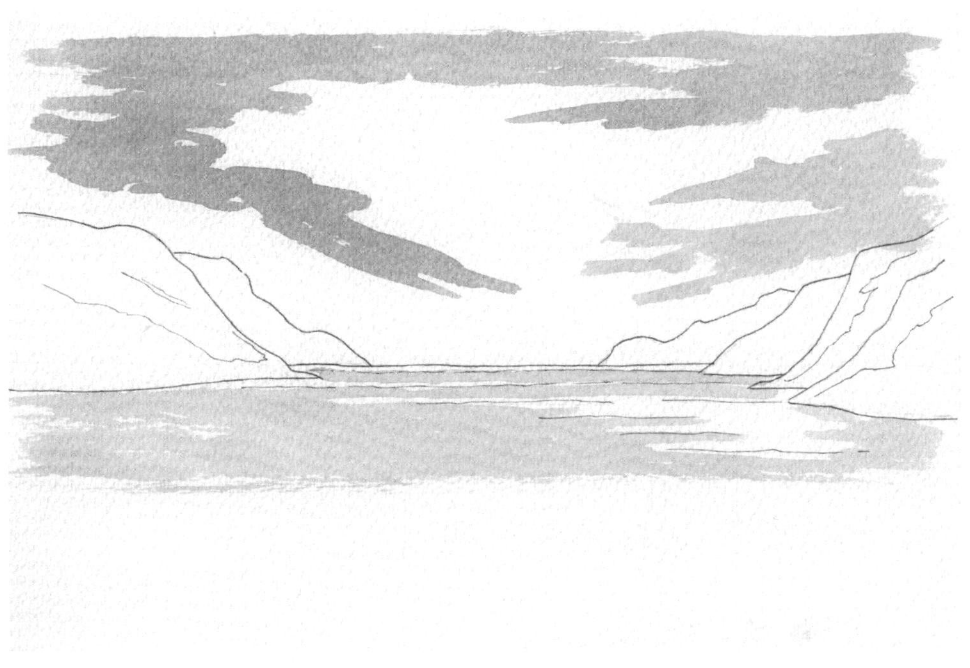

Loch Seaforth marks the border where Lewis gives way to Harris. The fjord-like sea loch cuts deep into the land and is a spectacular view in all weathers.

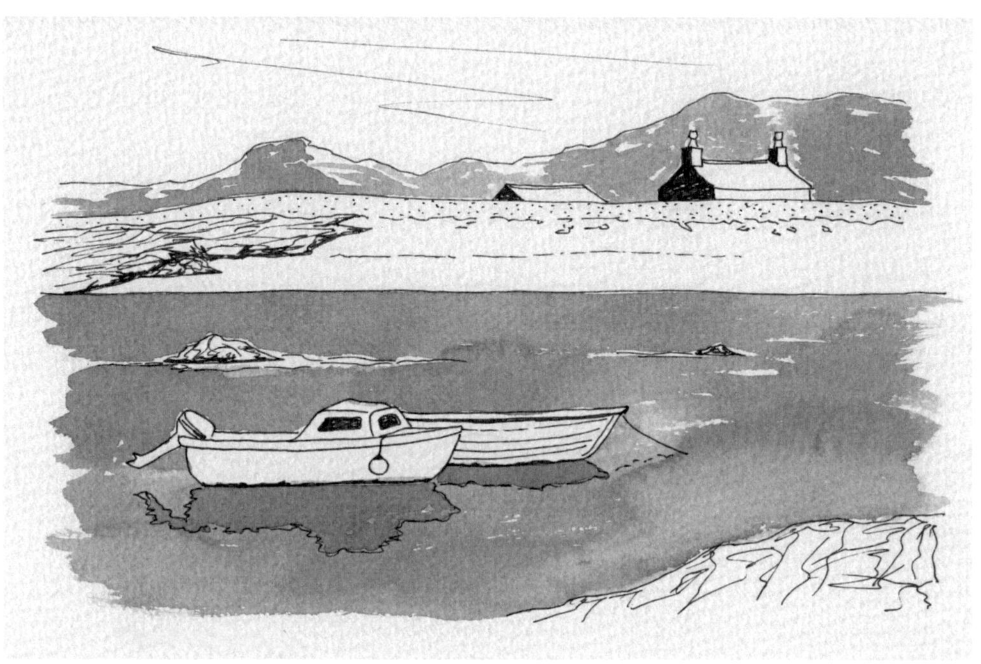

Boats, Kneep.

Uig and Great Bernera

THE UIG DISTRICT covers a vast area, which includes the island of Great Bernera, stretching from the mountains forming the border with Harris in the south, to Lochganvich in the Lewis interior. The area has diverse scenery and is known for its many stunning beaches, particularly on the Valtos peninsula and at Ardroil, where the Lewis Chessmen were found, hidden in a sand dune, in 1831. Made of walrus ivory and whale teeth, 11 of the 12th-century chessmen are kept at the National Museum of Scotland in Edinburgh and 82 at the British Museum in London.

Just south of Garynahine, a single track road leads to the island of Great Bernera. This small island is linked to Lewis by a short metal bridge known locally as 'The Bridge Over the Atlantic'. The bridge was constructed in 1953 after the people of Bernera threatened to take matters into their own hands by dynamiting the cliffs to form a causeway to Lewis.

Diary entry: A power cut on Christmas Day due to power lines being damaged by strong wind. Some friends call around (who usually go away for Christmas) and we try to make the best of it by playing board games by candlelight. Not the Christmas Day that any of us had planned but enjoyable enough. However our friends vow never to spend Christmas on the island again.

Diary entry: An article in the press reports that the Thailand Tourist Board has used a photograph of a beach in the Outer Hebrides with white sand, turquoise sea and distant hills to promote its own resorts. A spokeswoman for VisitScotland is quoted as graciously saying that 'imitation is the sincerest form of flattery'.

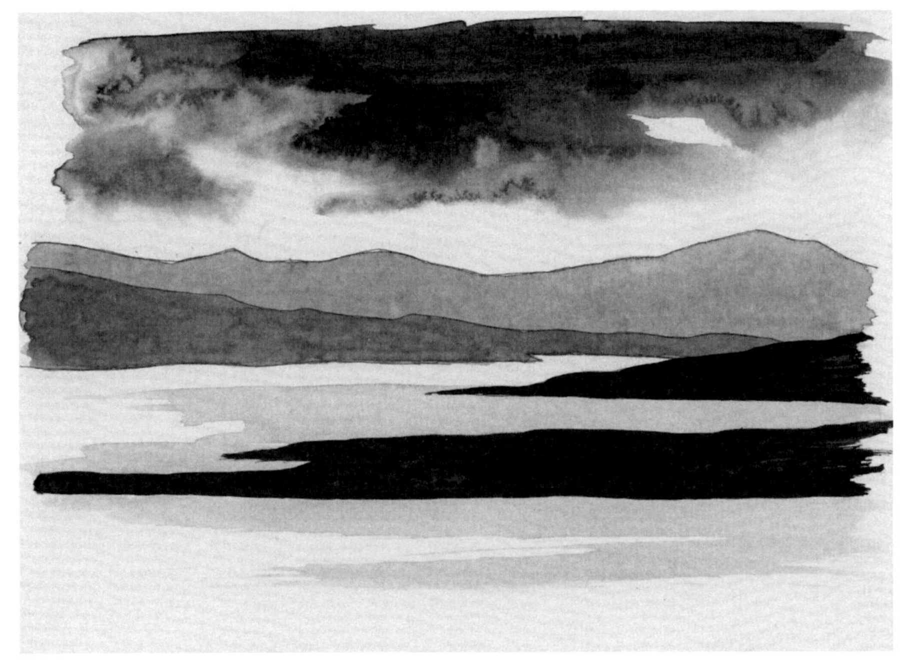

Uig hills.

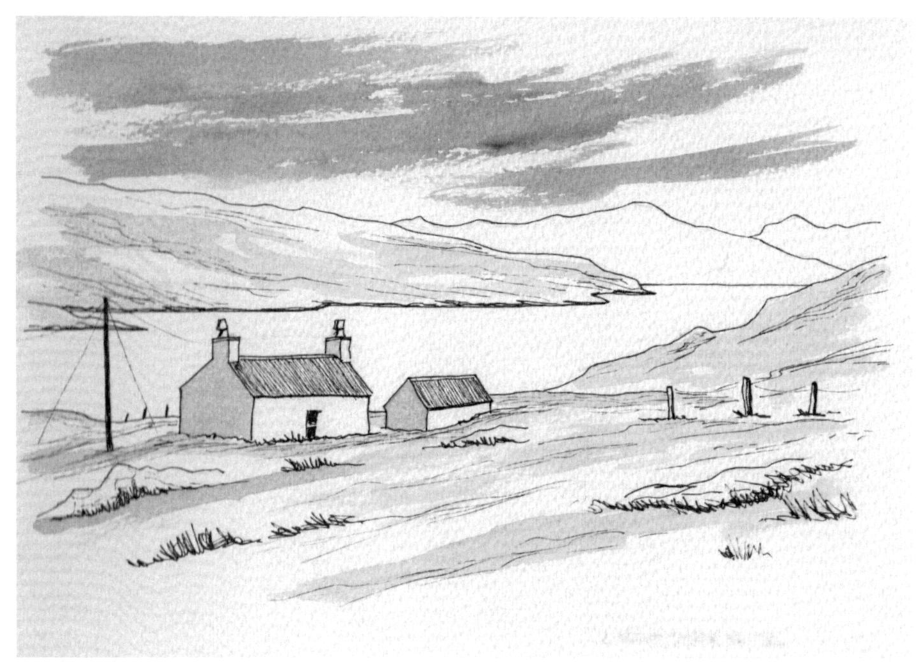

Little Loch Roag.

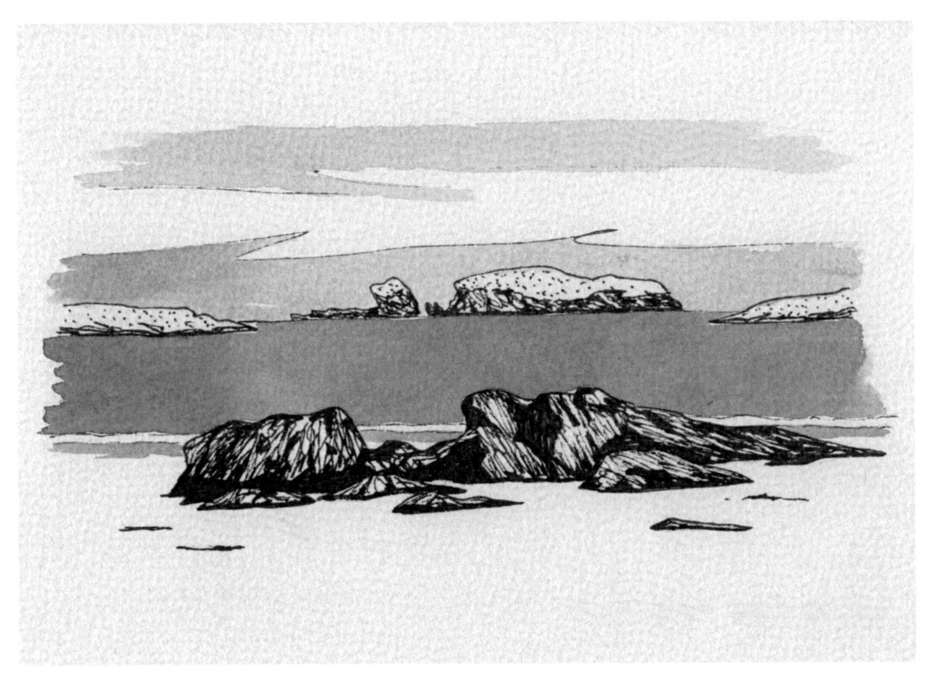

A cold, clear and crisp day, Bosta Beach, Great Bernera.

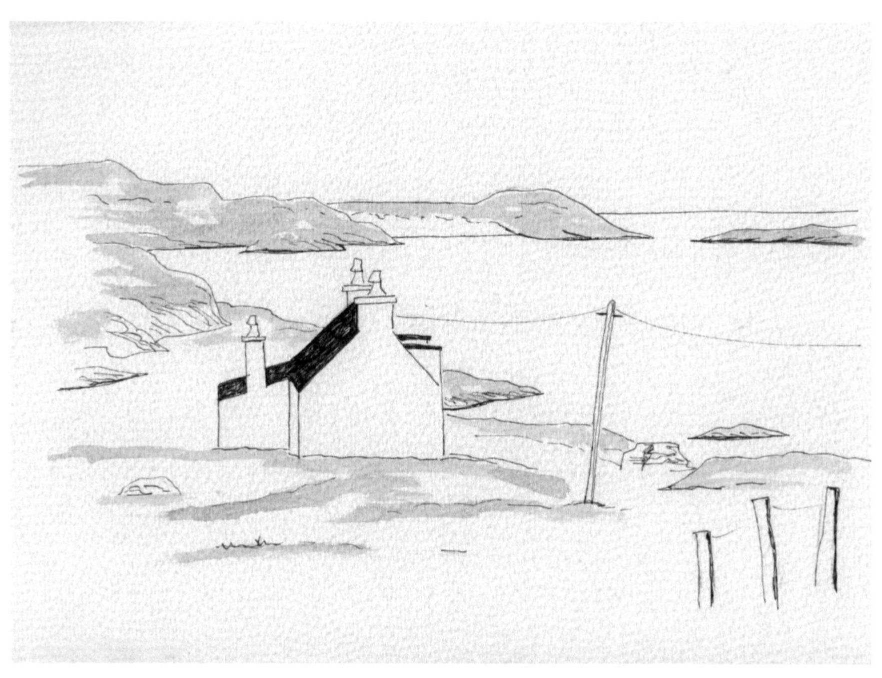

Crior, Great Bernera.

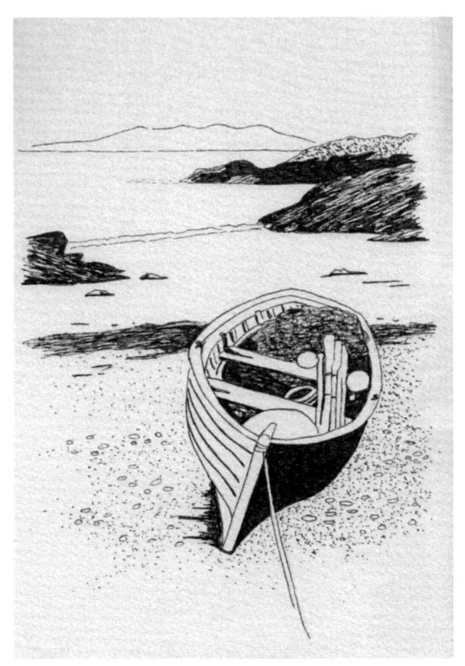

Tobson, Great Bernera.

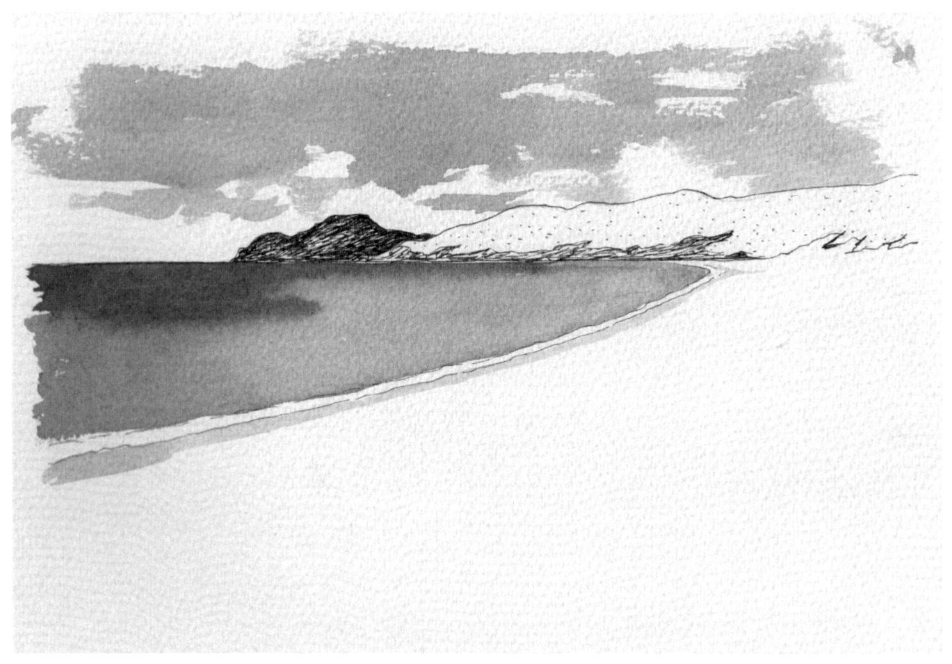

Cliff beach, as the name suggests, is surrounded by some of the highest cliffs on Lewis.

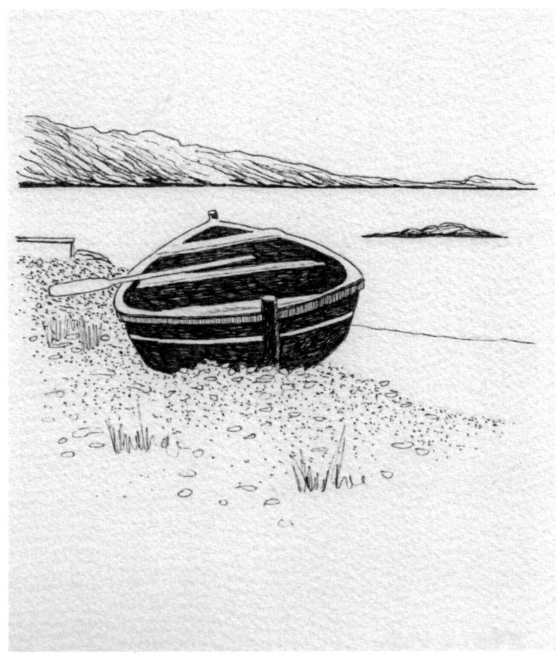

The Valtos loop road takes in small scattered communities and the beaches at Cliff, Valtos, Kneep (pictured) and Reef.

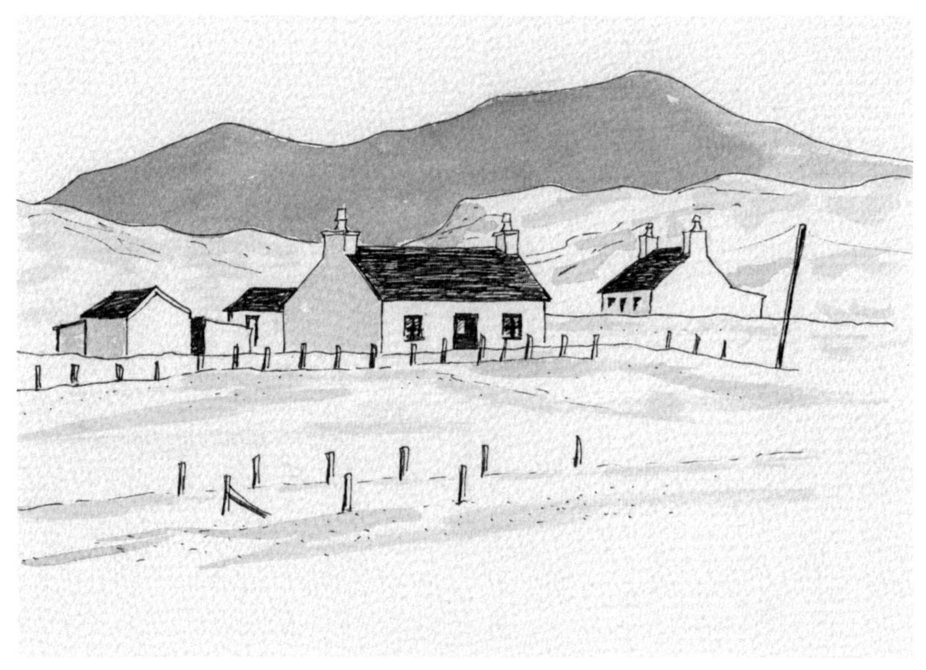

Crofts at Ardroil.

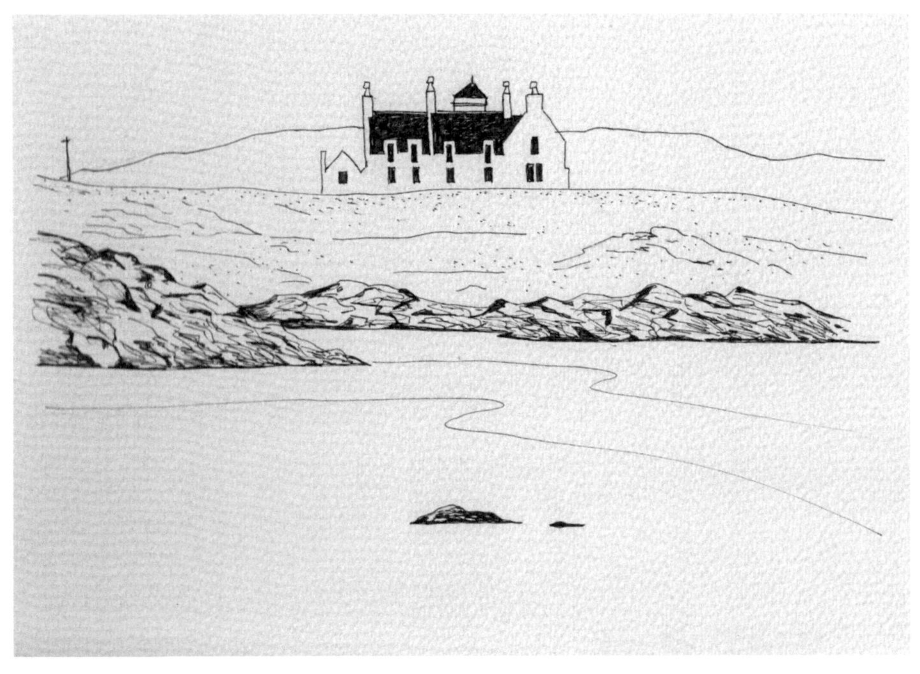

Uig Lodge, Timsgarry. Built in 1876 and once owned by Lord Leverhulme.

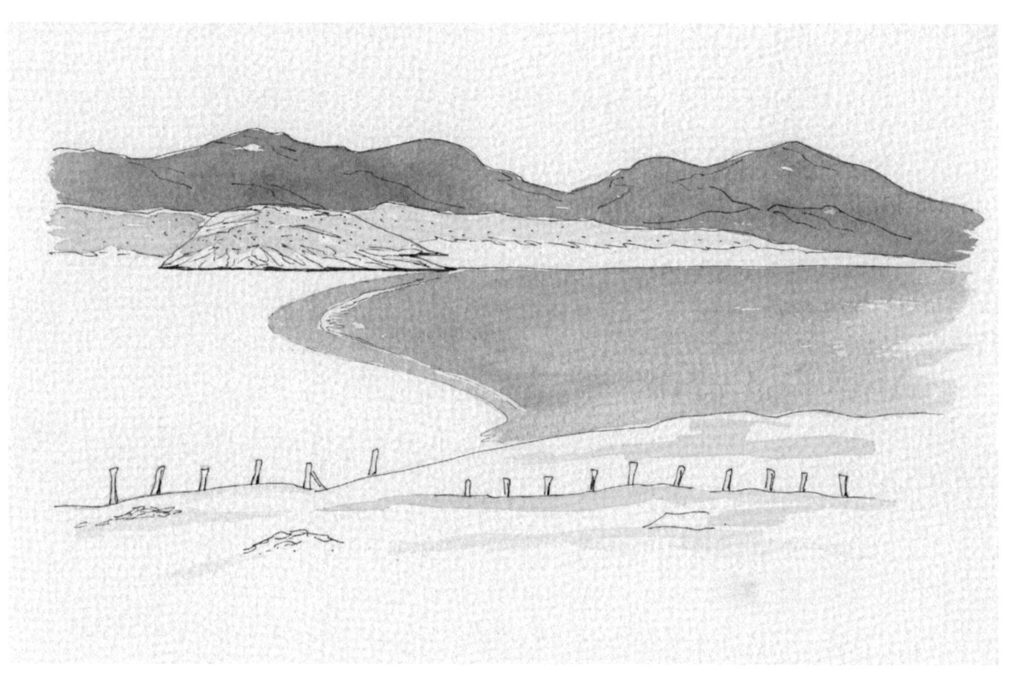

Uig sands from Timsgarry. At low tide the sea can be as much as a mile away.

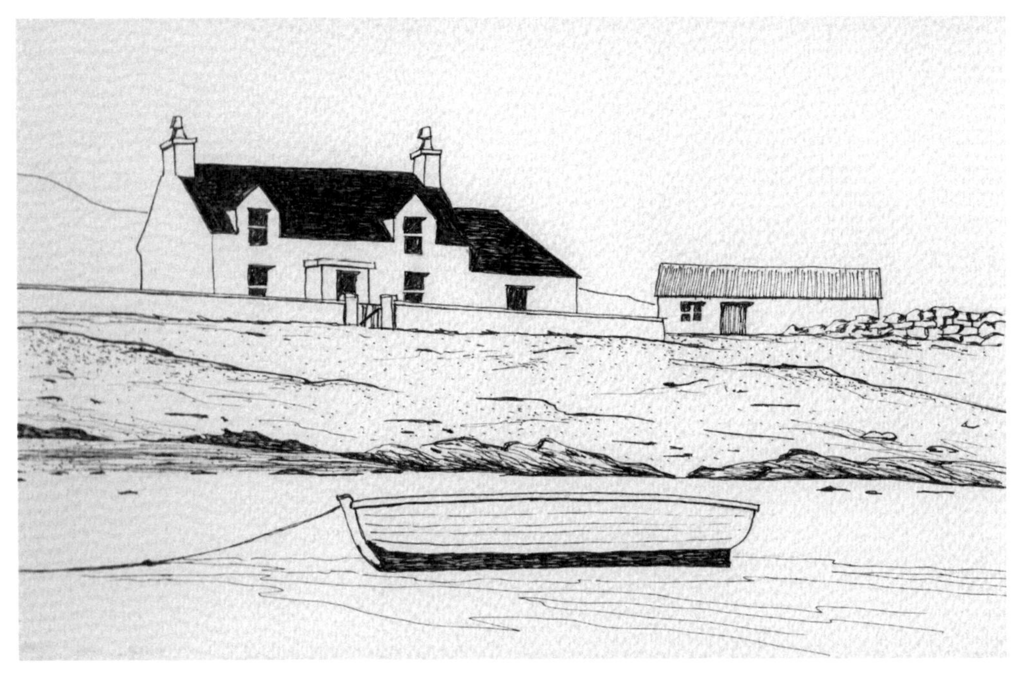

Carnish, Uig sands.

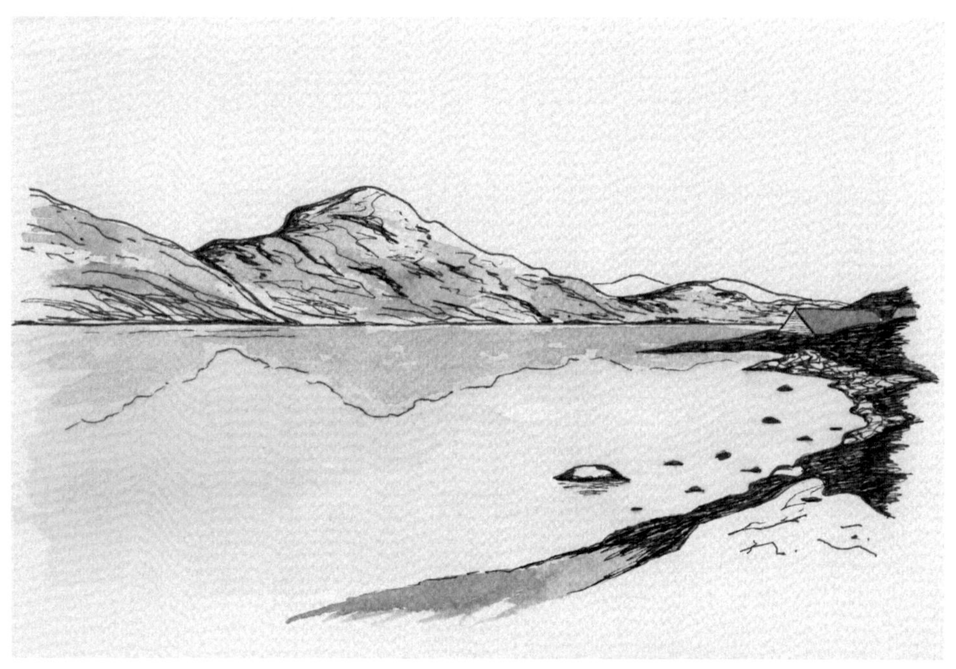

Loch Suinaval.

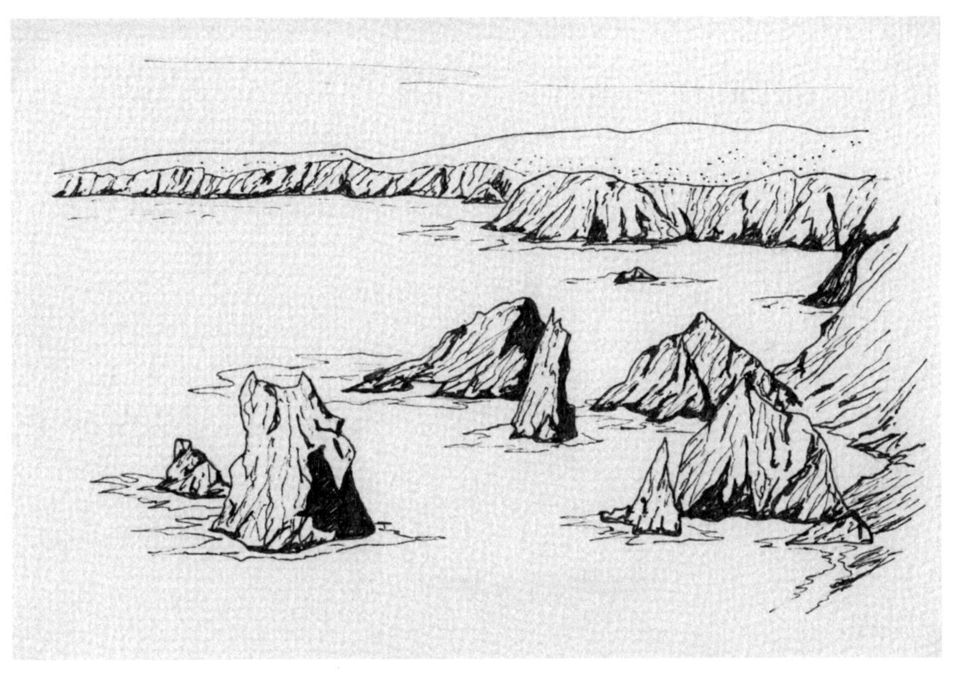

Sea stacks, Mangersta. The single track road meanders on for around eight miles from Mangersta until it gives up the ghost and turns into a track at Mealista.

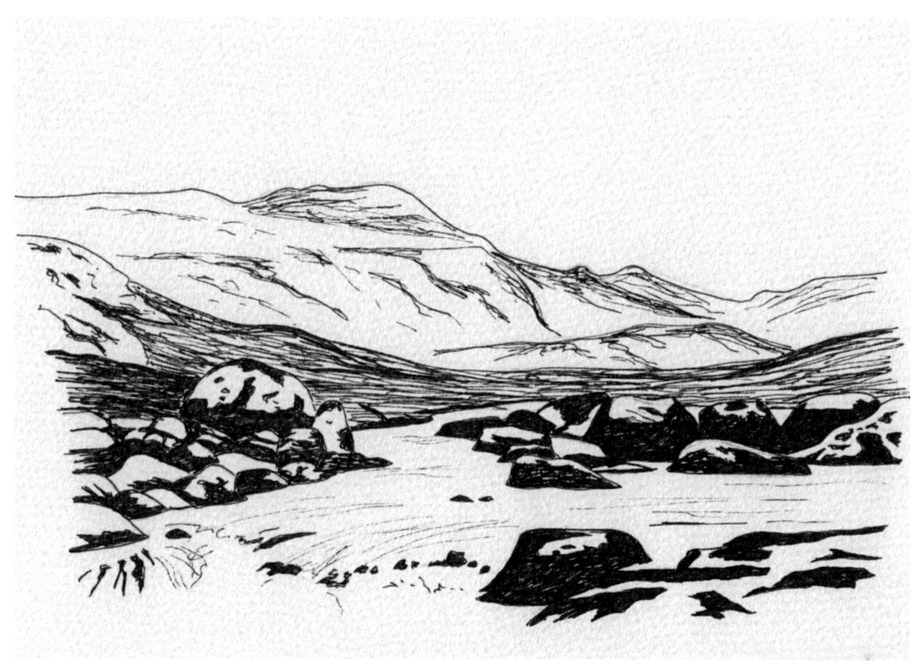

The Clisham.

North Harris

THE A859 ROAD from Lewis crosses into Harris at Aline Lodge by the shore of Loch Seaforth. In the 1990s large sections of this road were still single track with passing places all the way to the Hushinish road junction. In recent years the road has been substantially upgraded in line with others on the island, with the help of EU funding. North Harris is wild, remote, mountainous terrain and is very sparsely populated. Among the many hills is the Clisham, which at 799m is the highest mountain not only in Lewis and Harris but in the whole of the Outer Hebrides. Tarbert, the capital of Harris, is situated on an isthmus between West and East Loch Tarbert and has the ferry terminal, some small shops, hotels and a newly built distillery.

Diary entry: I mention the poor state of part of the A859 road from Ardvourlie to Ardhasaig in North Harris and get a humorous reply. 'It's supposed to be an A road, when it is barely just a road,' comments my neighbour.

Diary entry: An interesting conversation in the gallery today between two couples who are touring the islands in campervans. Comparing notes, one couple highly recommend Hushinish, but the other couple are quick to reply that they have already been and would never go back again. It turns out that they stayed three nights in Hushinish when they only intended to stay for one. They go on to explain that they needed the extra nights to pluck up the courage to make the 15 mile return journey to the A859, leaving their spot by the beach at 5.00am, with fingers crossed that no one else would be on the road so early. I do have some sympathy, as this is a tortuous route with twists and turns, blind summits, sharp climbs and descents that make for a rollercoaster ride. As they leave, I catch sight of their very large rented campervan, which explains their nervousness.

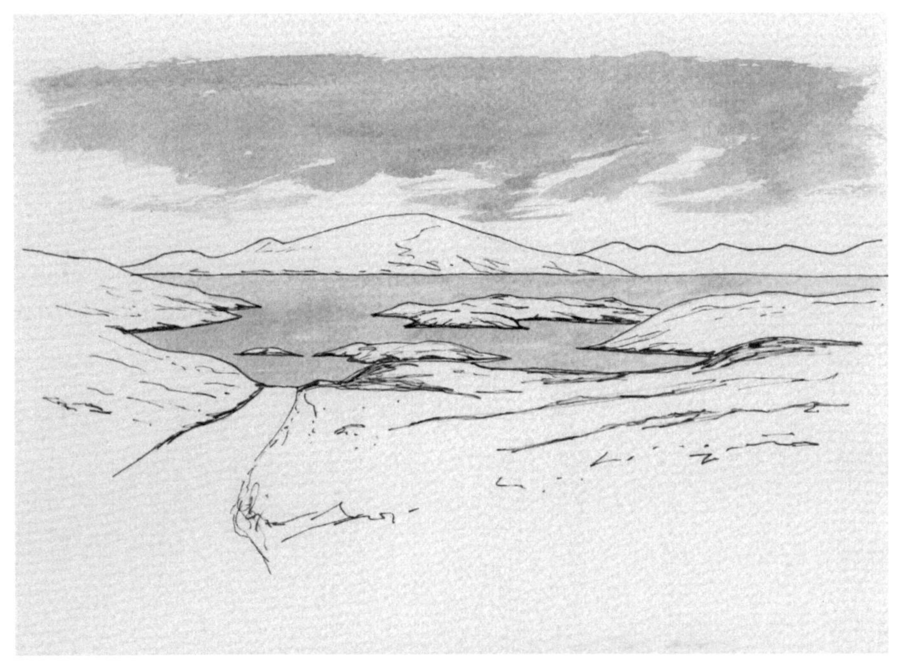

West Loch Tarbert.

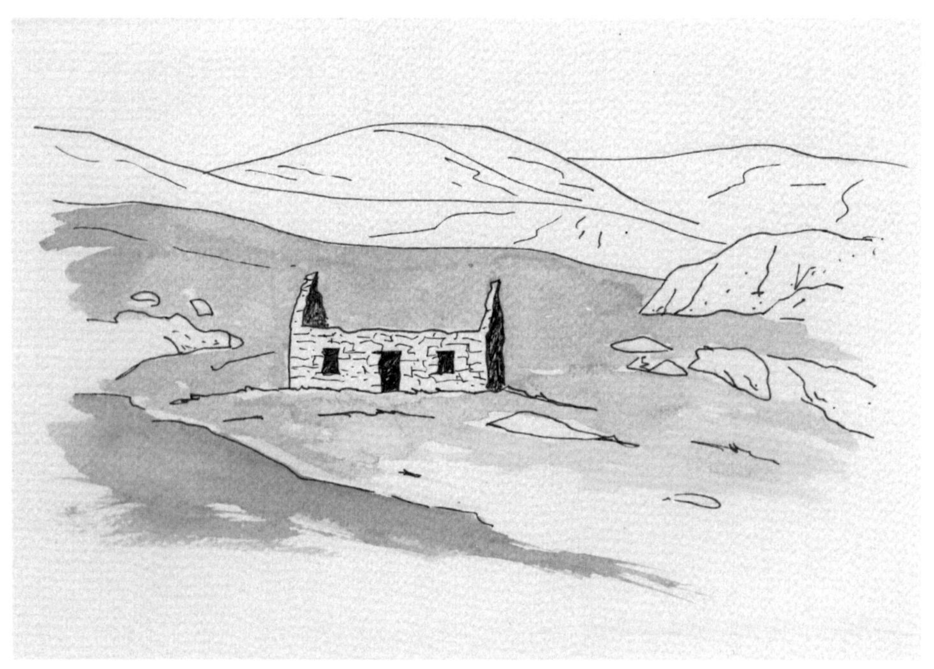

Ruin in the hills, North Harris.

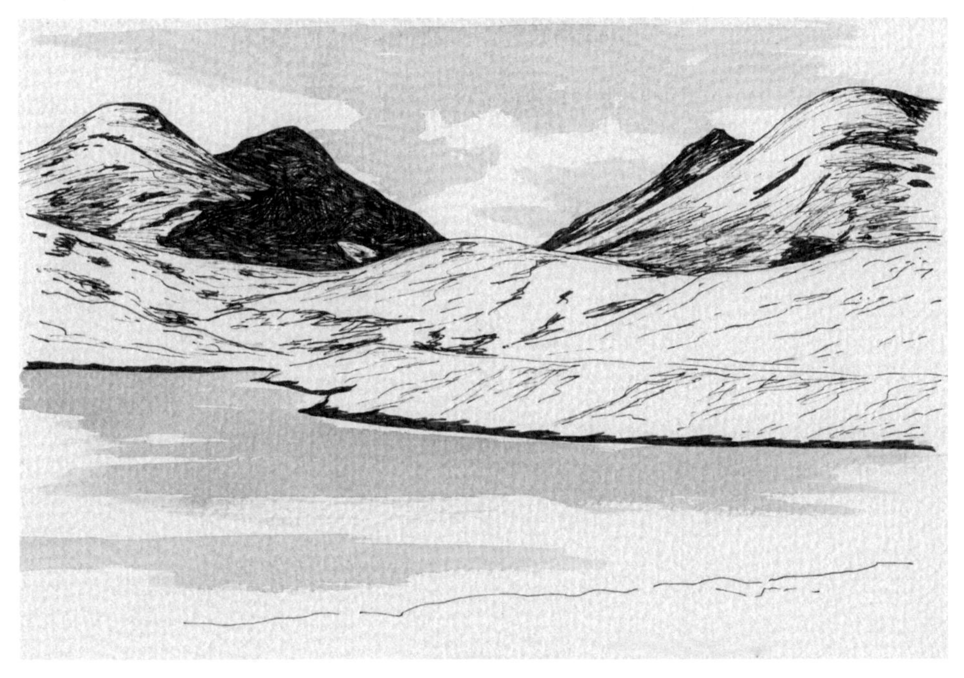

North Harris hills.

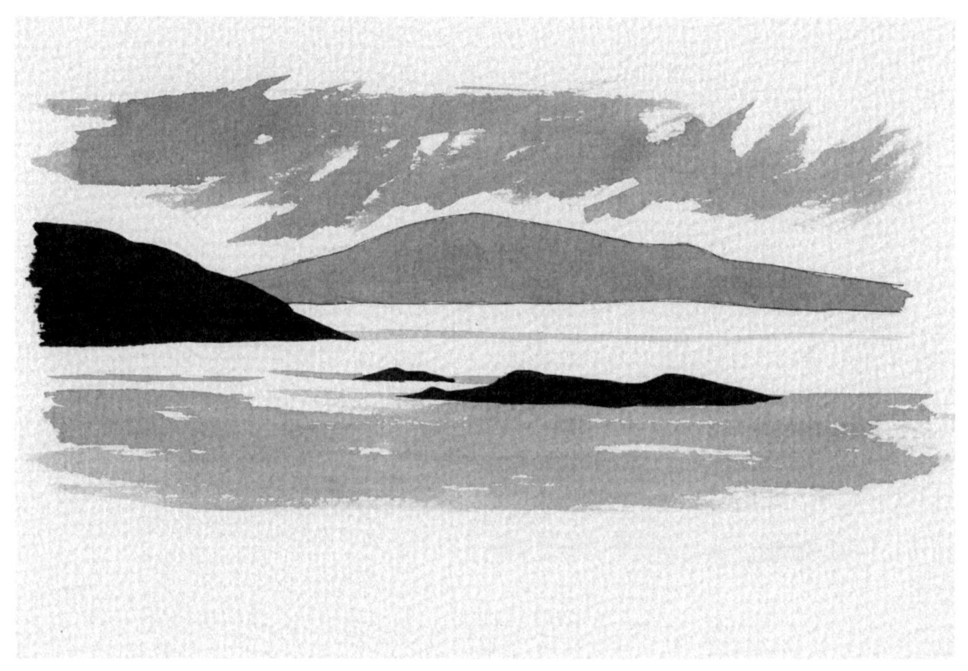

West Loch Tarbert light.

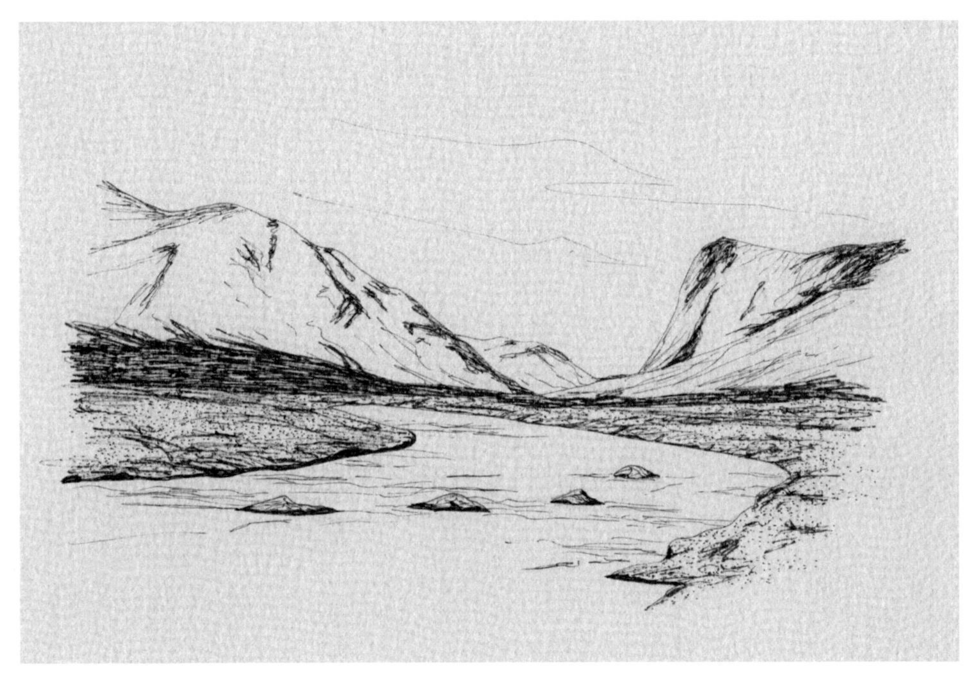

Glen Miavaig. Golden Eagle territory.

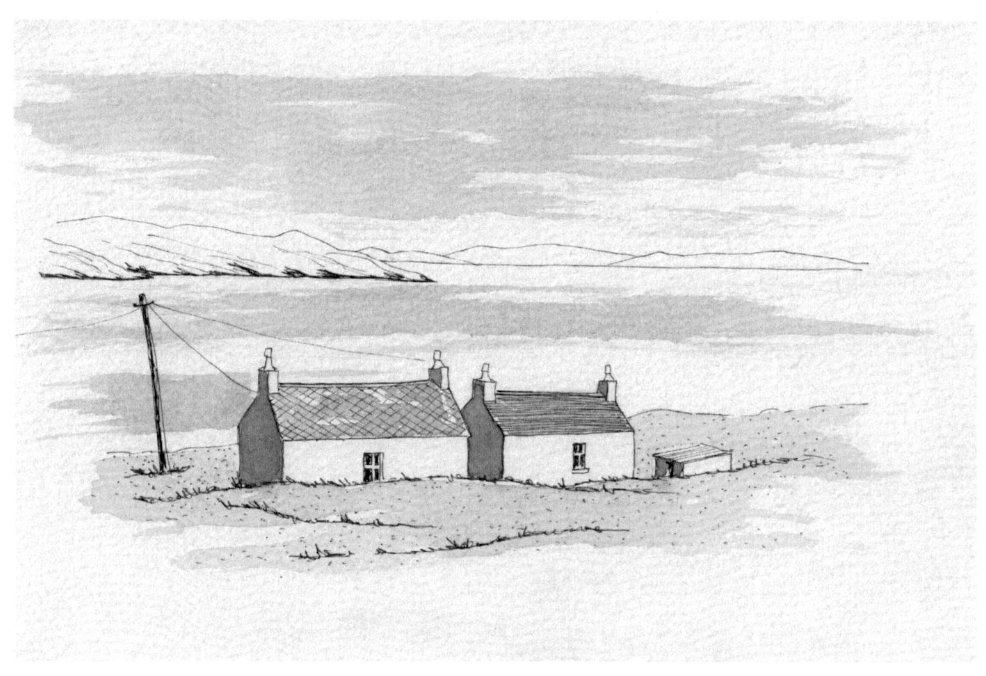

Hushinish.

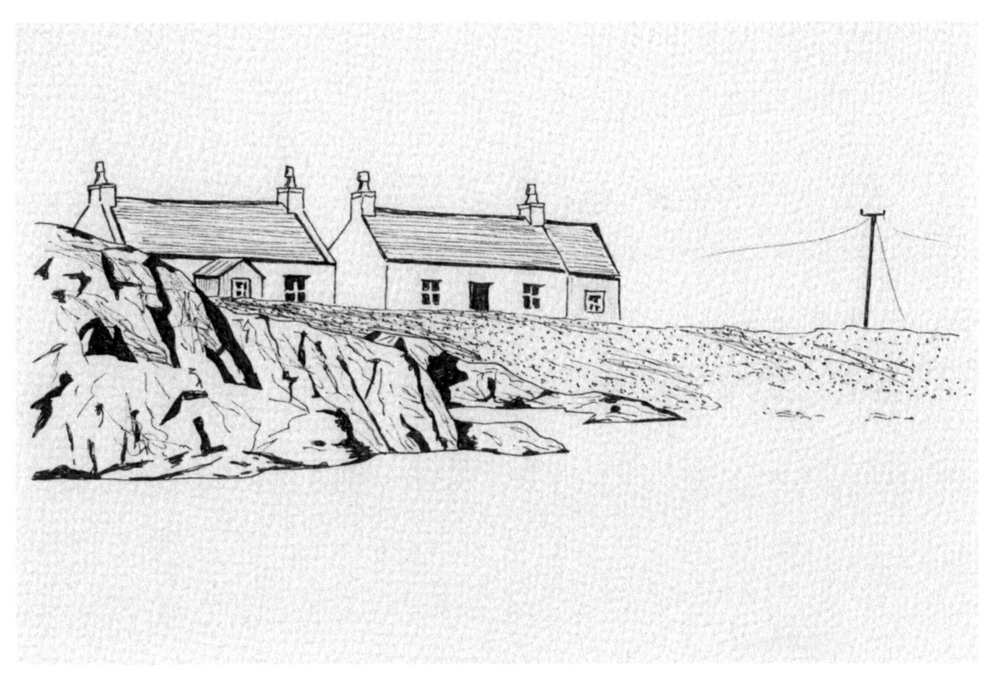

Beachside cottages, Hushinish.

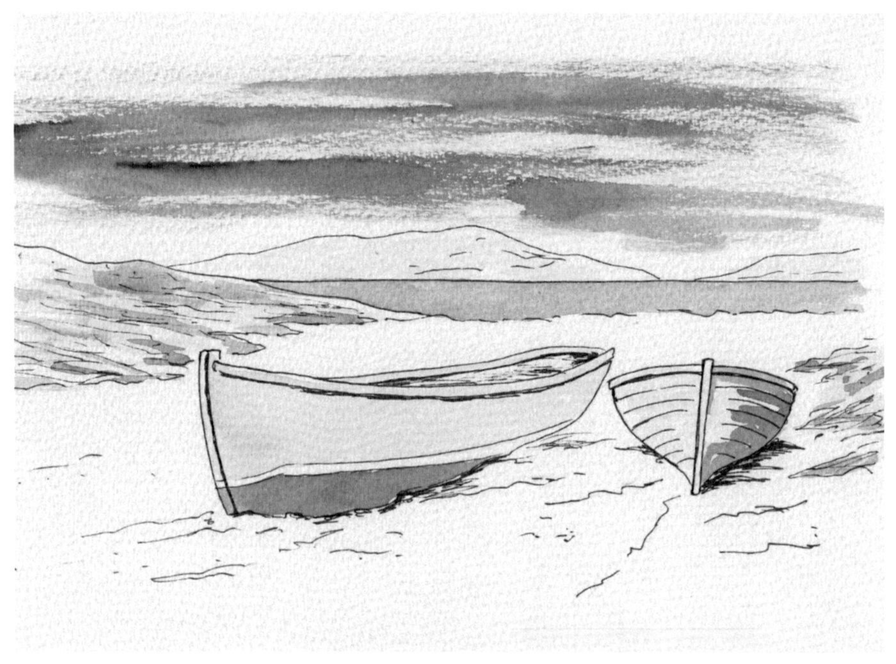

Beached boats by the Hushinish slipway looking across to the uninhabited Isle of Scarp.

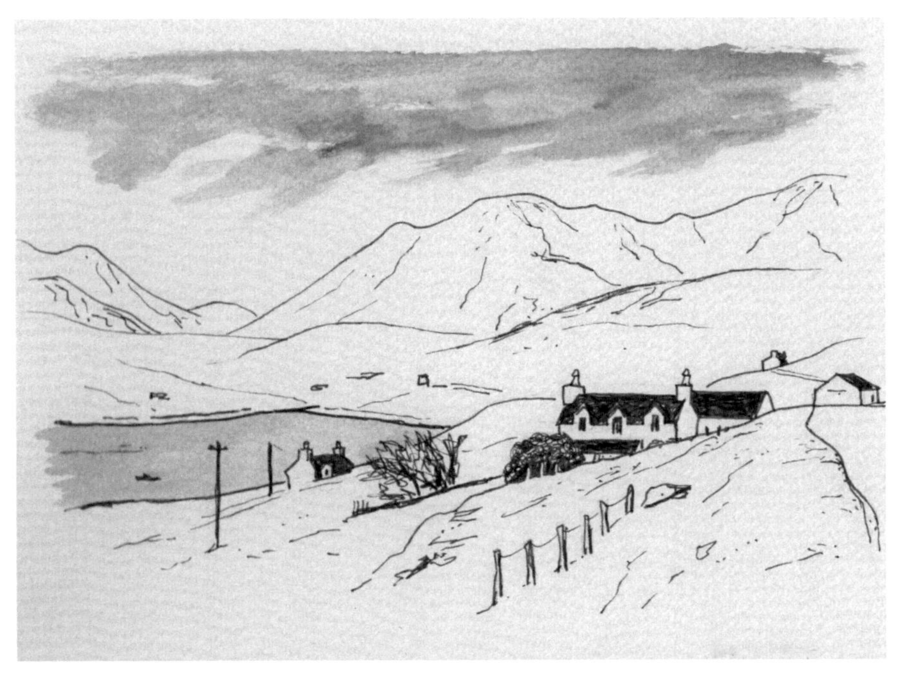

North Harris hills from Ardhasaig.

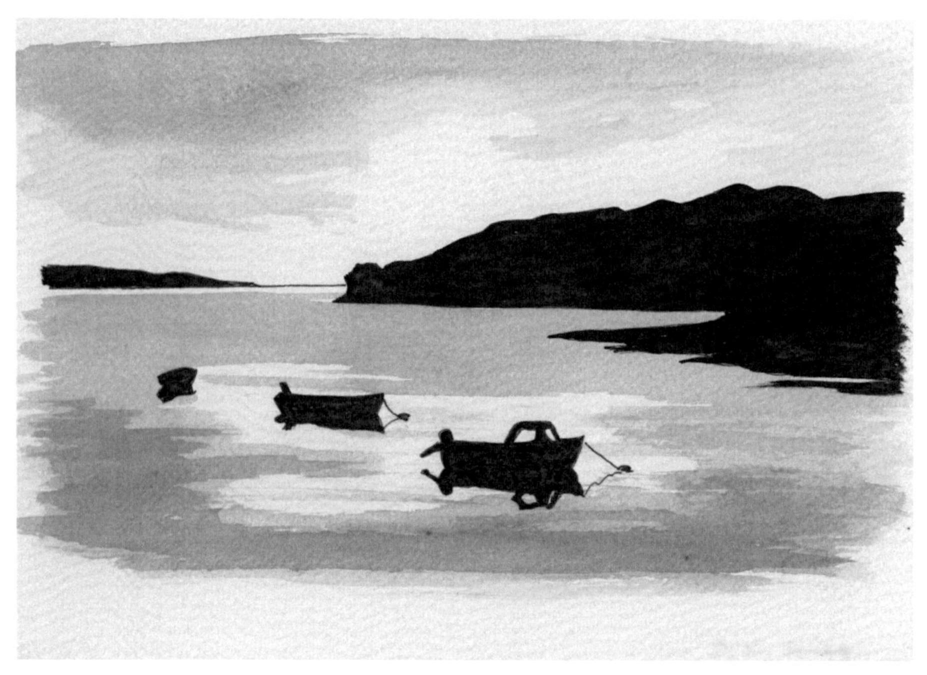

Boats, Tarbert.

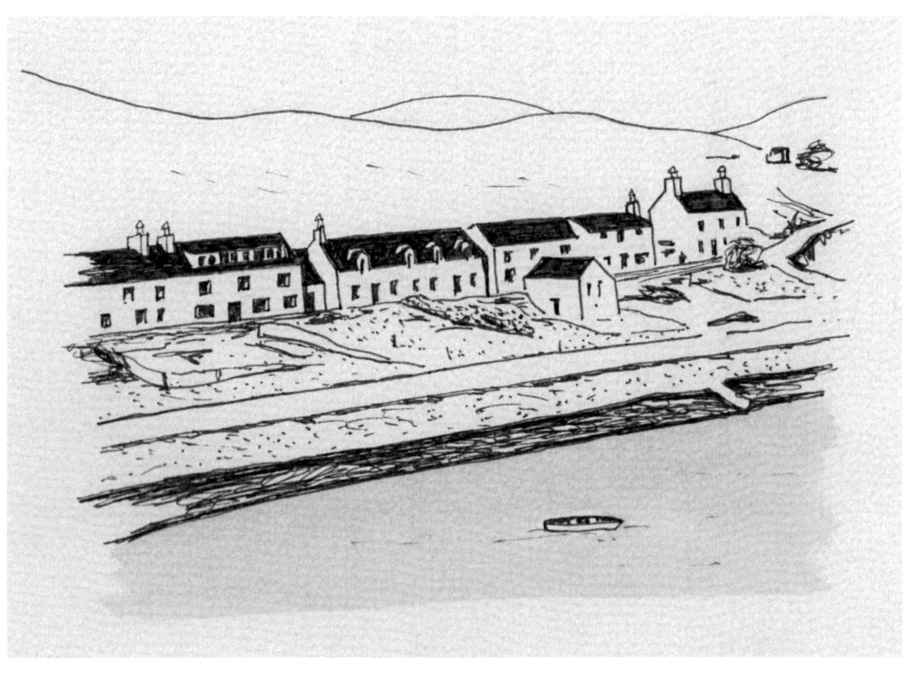

Tarbert.

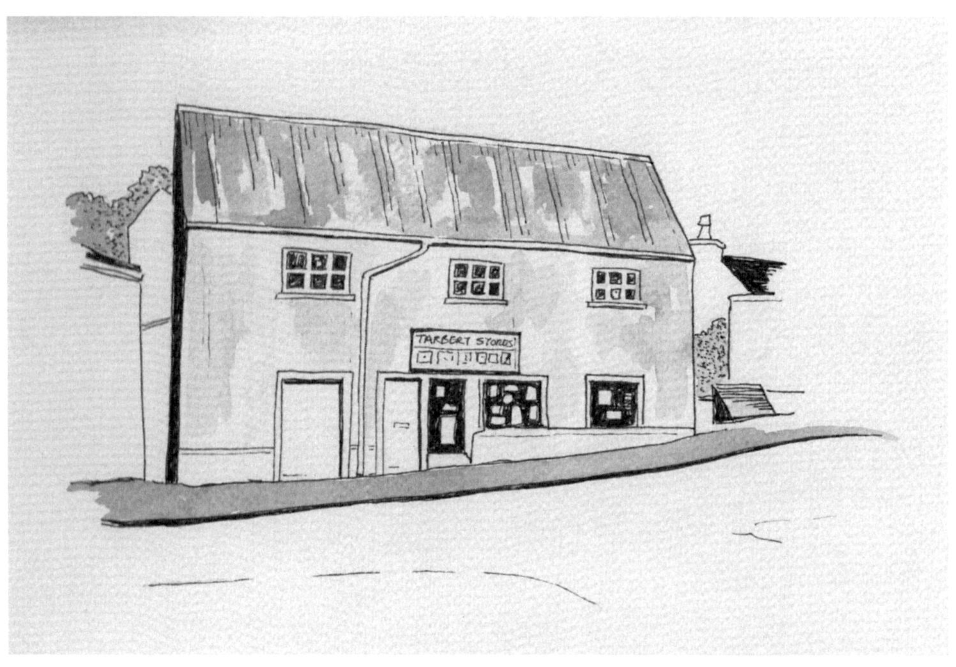

Tarbert Stores. A characterful DIY and hardware store stocking everything for the homeowner, crofter and fisherman.

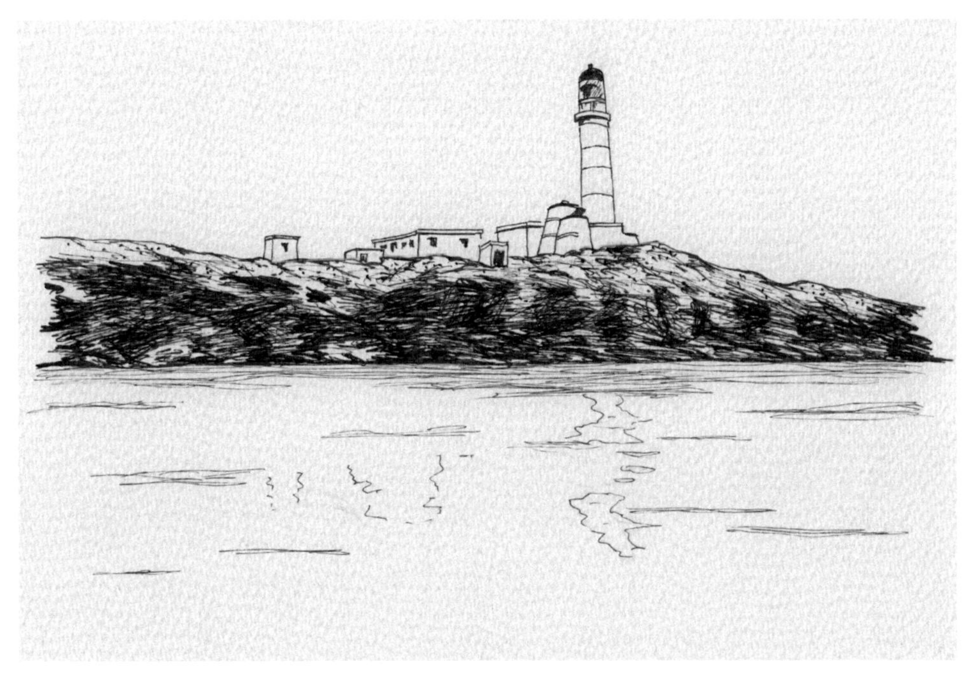

Eilean Glas lighthouse, Scalpay.

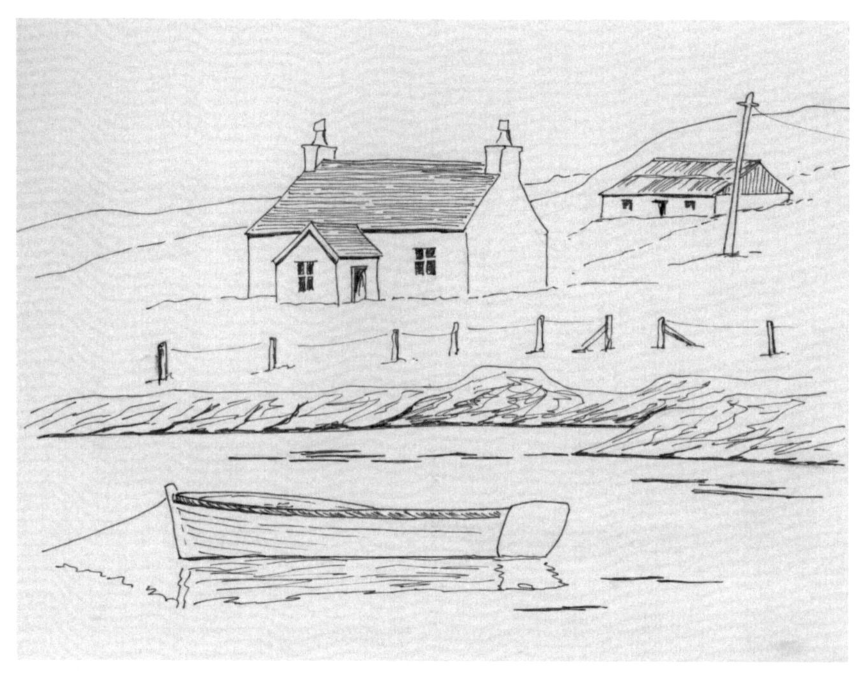

Scalpay. This small island has been linked to Harris by a road bridge since 1997.

South Harris

South Harris is a land of contrasts. The meandering C79 single track road which runs through the Bays area on the east coast is known as the 'Golden Road'. The inference being that it was so named because it took so long and cost so much to build. The first impression of the east coast Bays is of bare rock, lochs and very little vegetation. The west coast is completely different. A series of stunning beaches, all revealed one after another from the road, with sand dunes, machair (grassland and wildflower pasture) and impressive hills as a backdrop. The white shell sand and Caribbean coloured sea give the Harris beaches near legendary status that sees them regularly top polls as the most beautiful in the UK and even the world.

Diary entry: There is a rumour circulating that four people from the BBC series Castaway *have been spotted shopping in Stornoway. It is the early stage of filming this social experiment on the Island of Taransay, and as the programme name suggests, the participants are supposed to be marooned on the island and fending for themselves. Whether it is true or not, it is a good story.*

Diary entry: A pristine summer day so we take a picnic to Scarista. Despite the perfect weather there are no more than 15 people on the beach. Just as we are considering moving on, a German tourist asks if we would be offended if he and his three friends strip off and film themselves running naked into the sea. We move on.

Diary entry: On a Sunday trip to Harris we stop off at St Clements at Rodel. The church is empty so we climb to the top of the tower to take in the view. As we carefully descend the narrow ladders and steps some time later, we are surprised to hear choral singing. When we reach the bottom there are two American tourists belting out a hymn in the belief that they were the only people in the church.

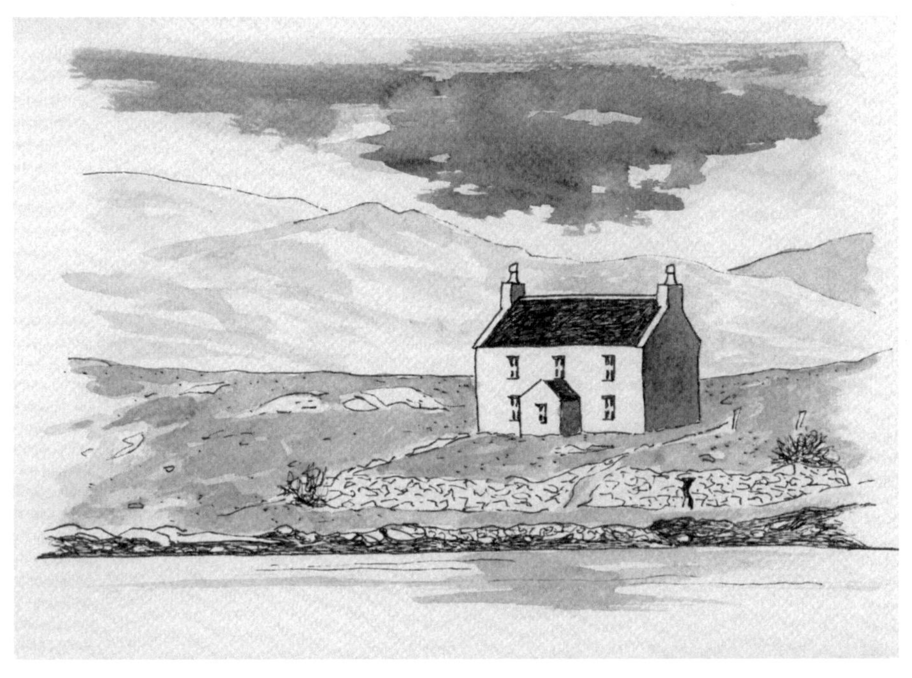

Manish, Bays.

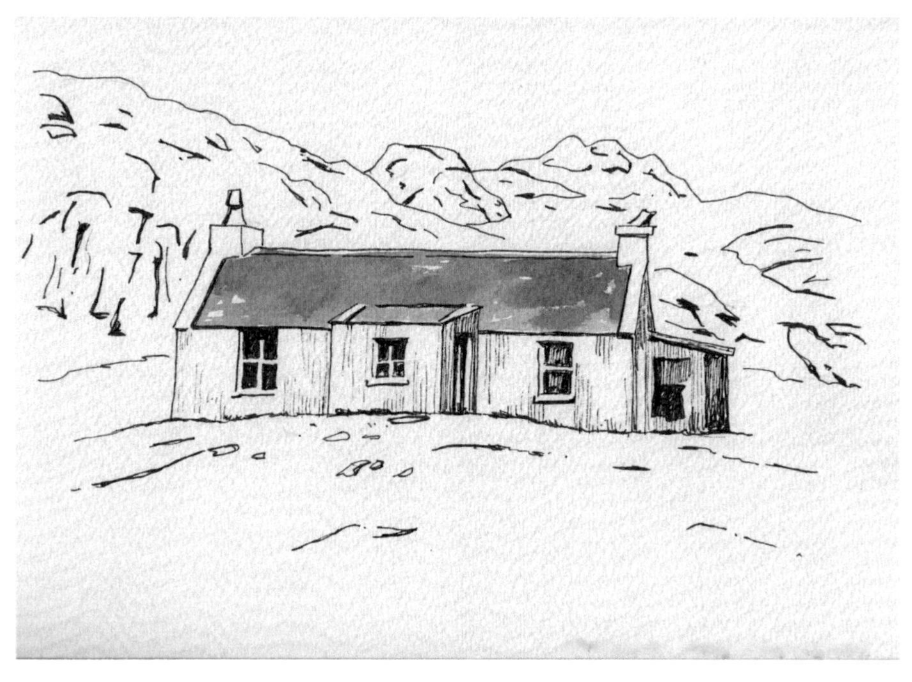

Abandoned croft, Drinishader.

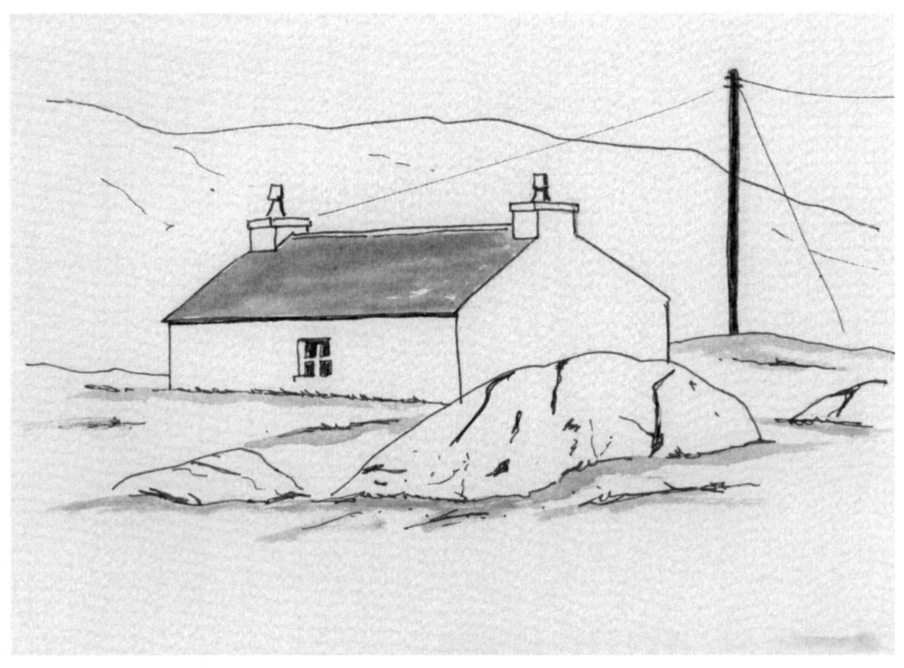

Stark bare rock and boulders in the Bays resemble a lunar landscape – Stanley Kubrick used the location to represent the surface of Jupiter in his film *2001: A Space Odyssey*.

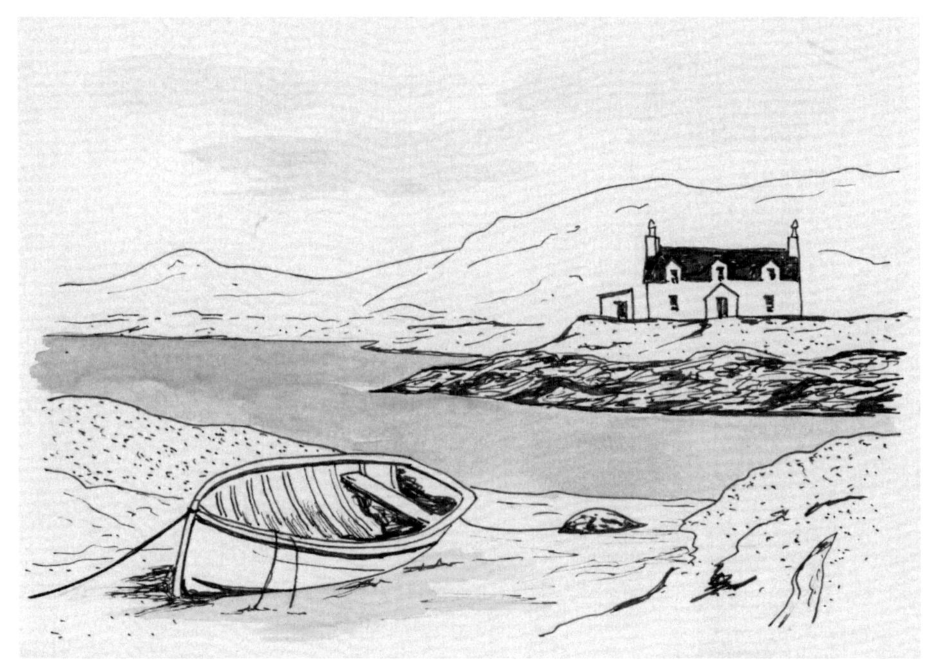

Low tide, Bays.

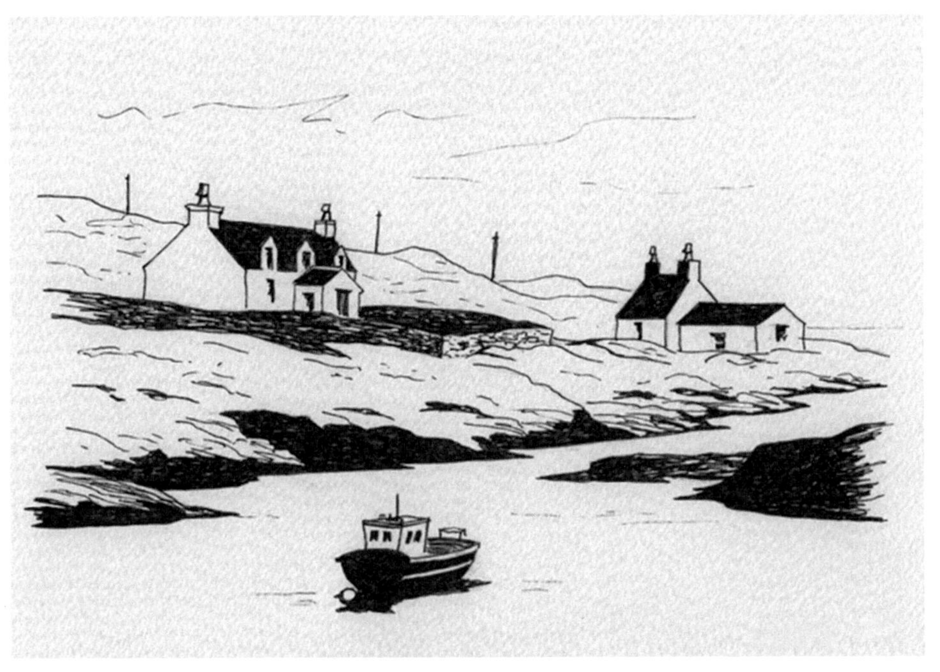

Finsbay, East Harris.

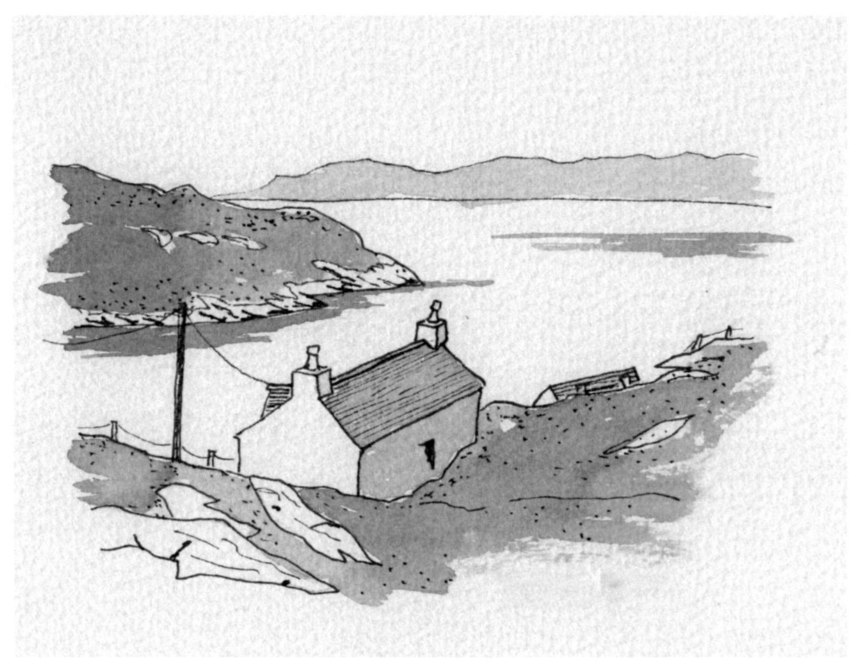

Geocrab, Bays.

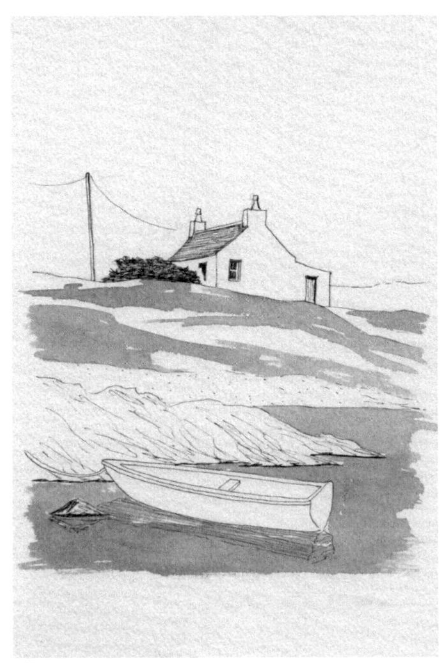

Boat and cottage, Finsbay.

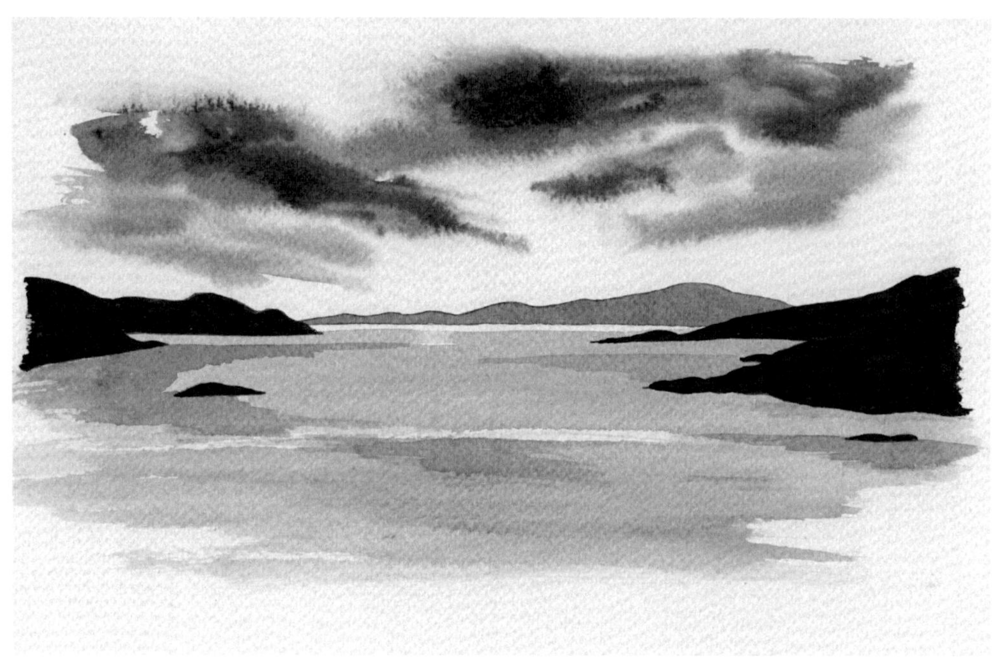

Island of Taransay.

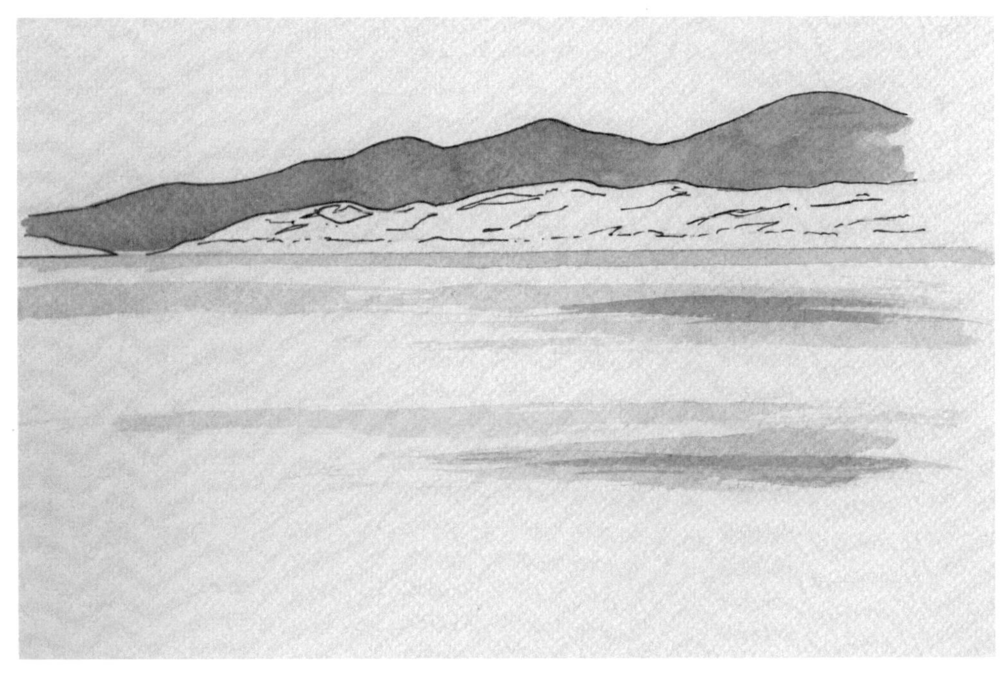

Low tide, Luskentyre.

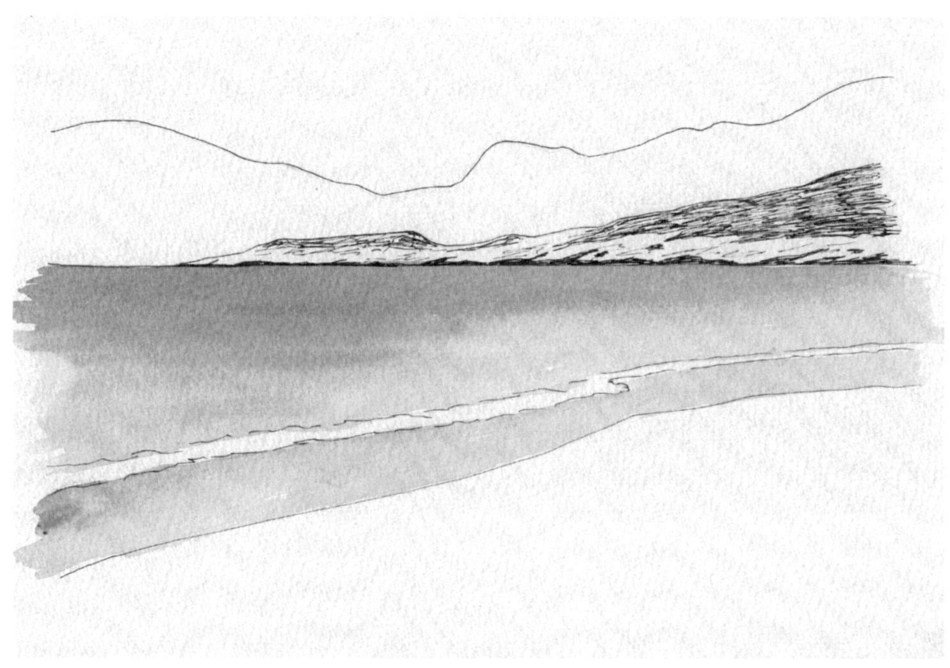

Luskentyre is often featured in articles and polls listing the 'best beaches in the world'. It is beautiful but in truth it is just one of the many stunning beaches in the Outer Hebrides.

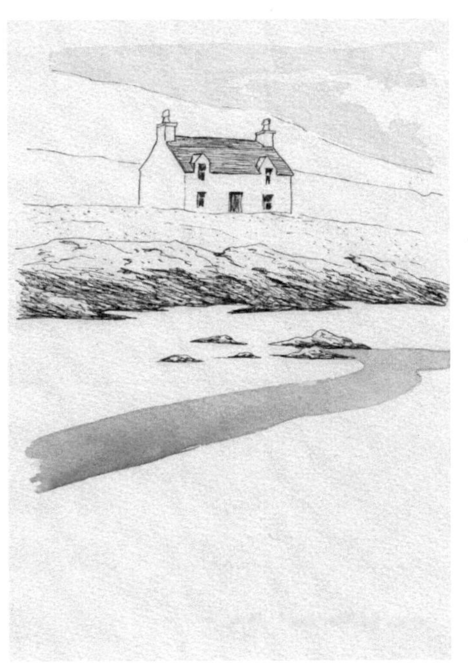

Beachside cottage, Luskentyre.

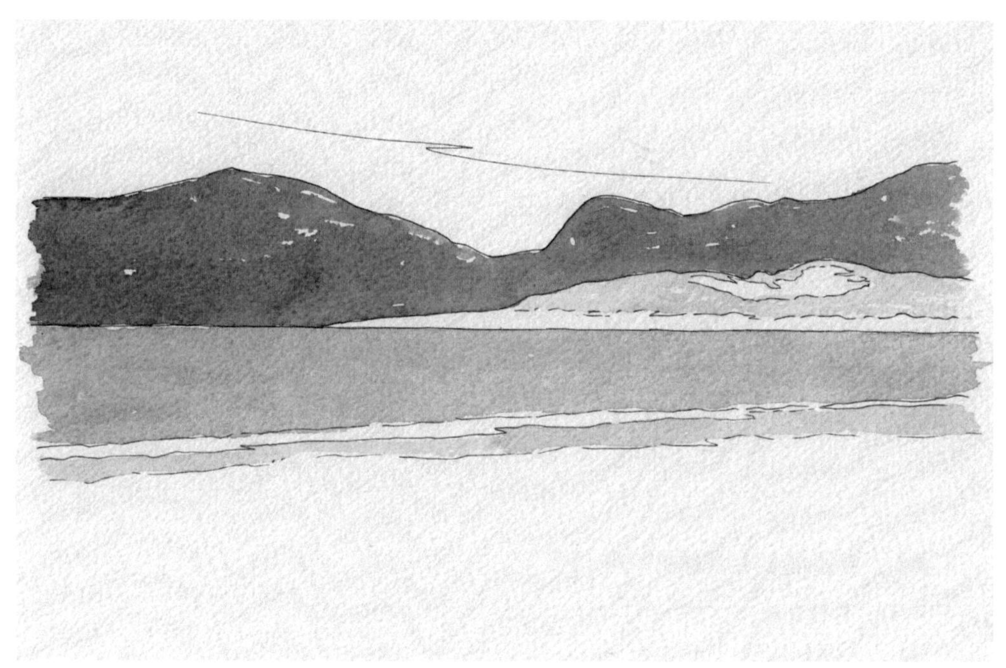

Luskentyre dunes from Horgabost.

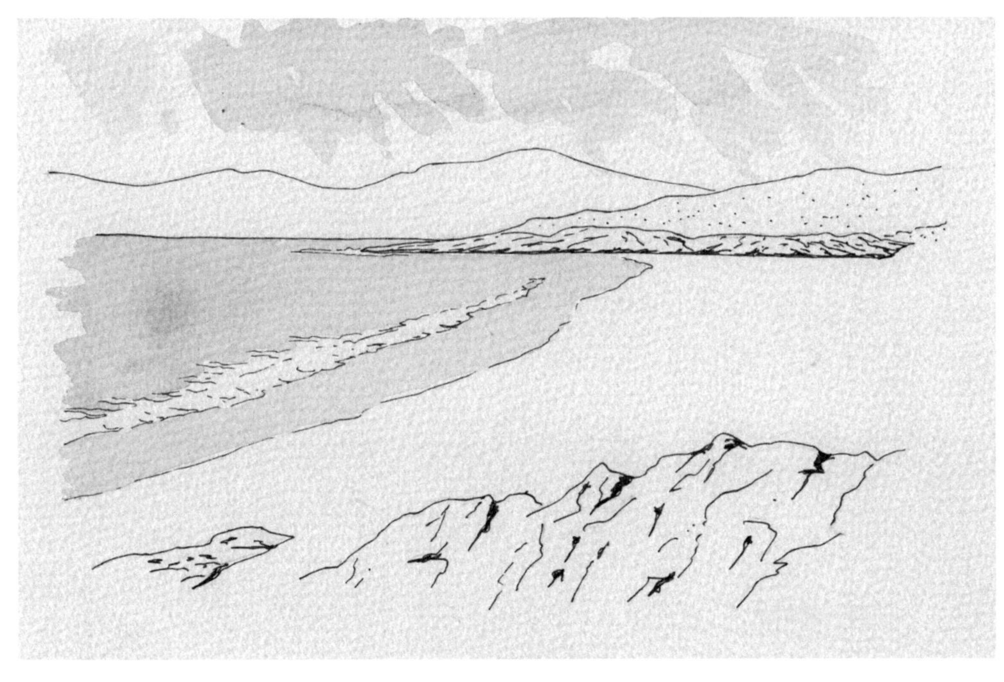

Nisabost beach.

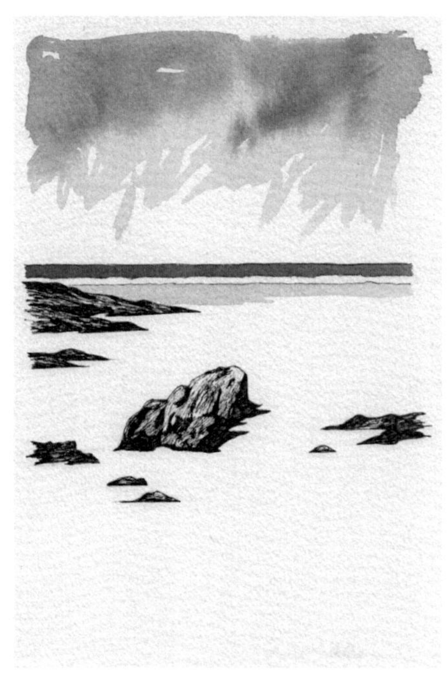

Borve beach.

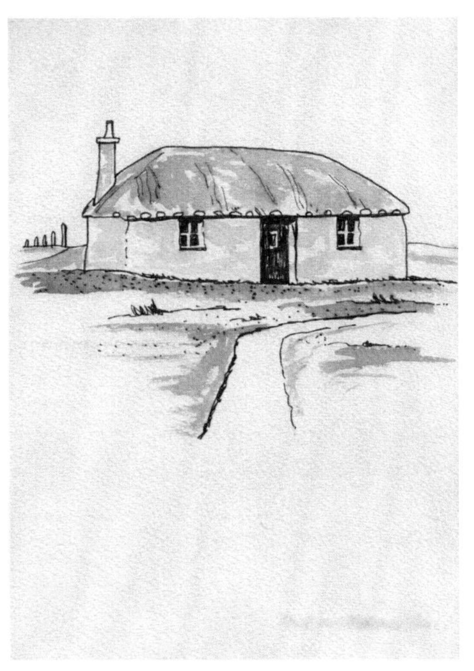

Thatched cottage, Borve.

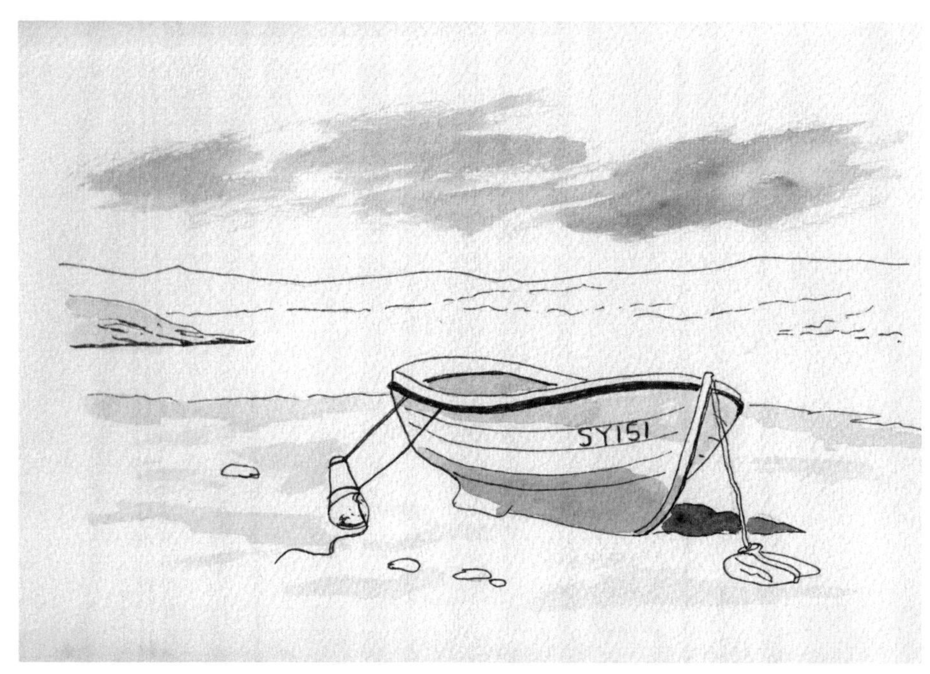

Tied-down boat, Seilebost.

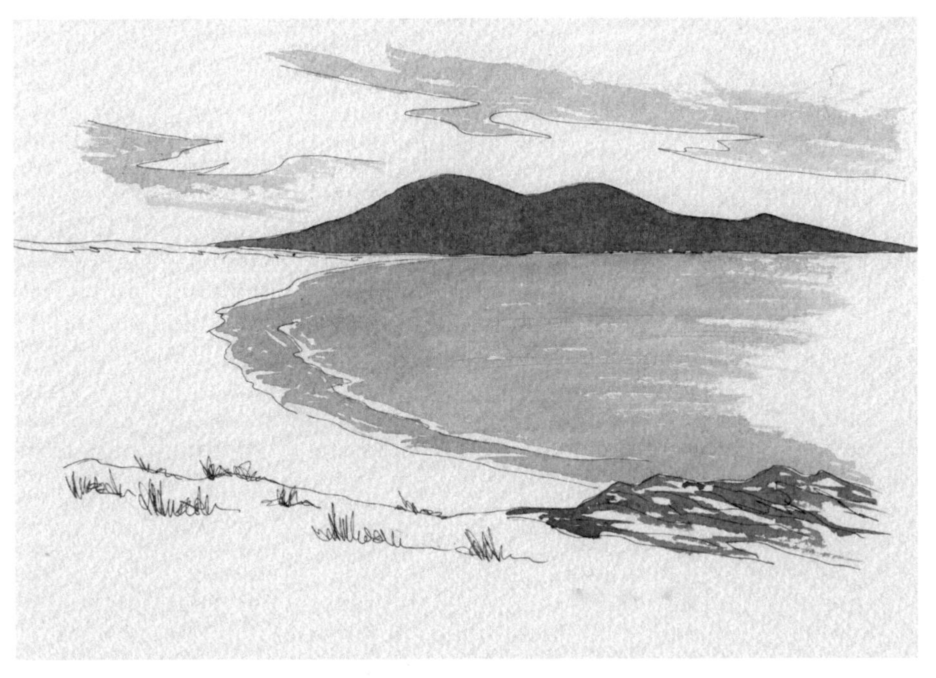

Scarista beach. Alongside the beach is the spectacularly sited Harris Golf Course.

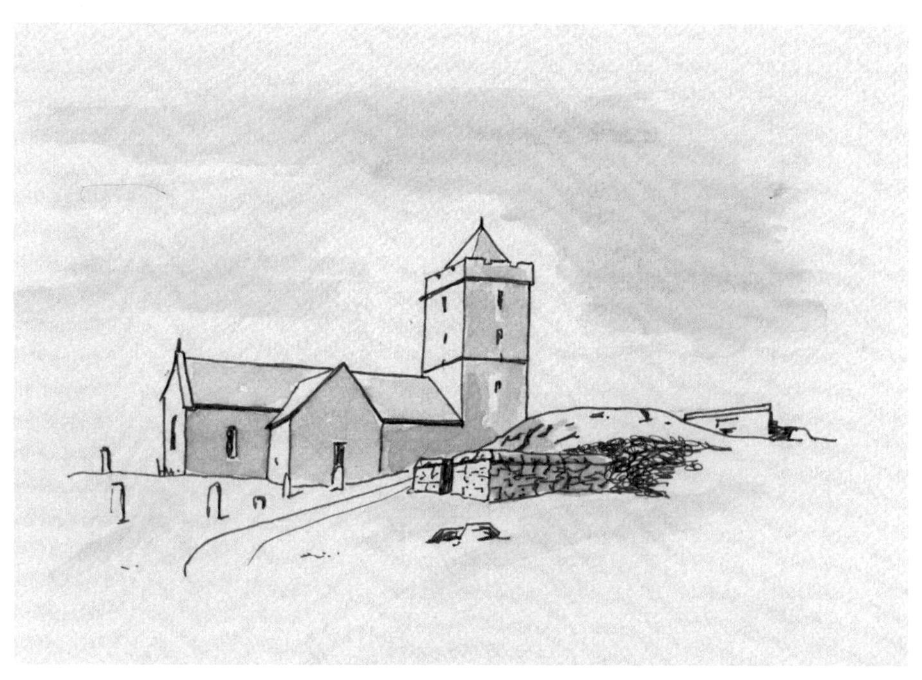

Rodel. Formerly the historic capital of Harris and main port.

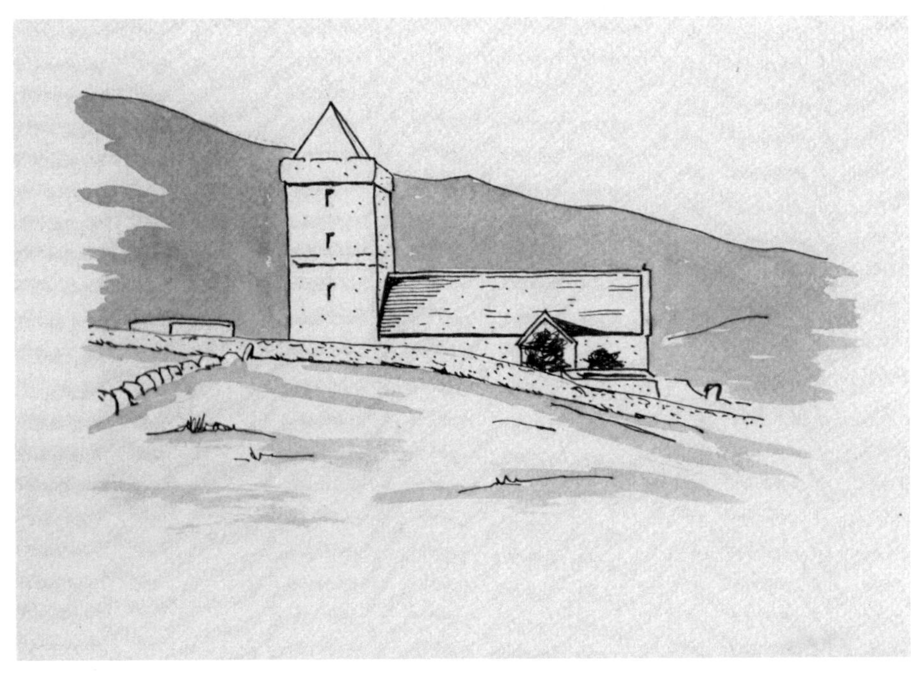

St Clements, Rodel.

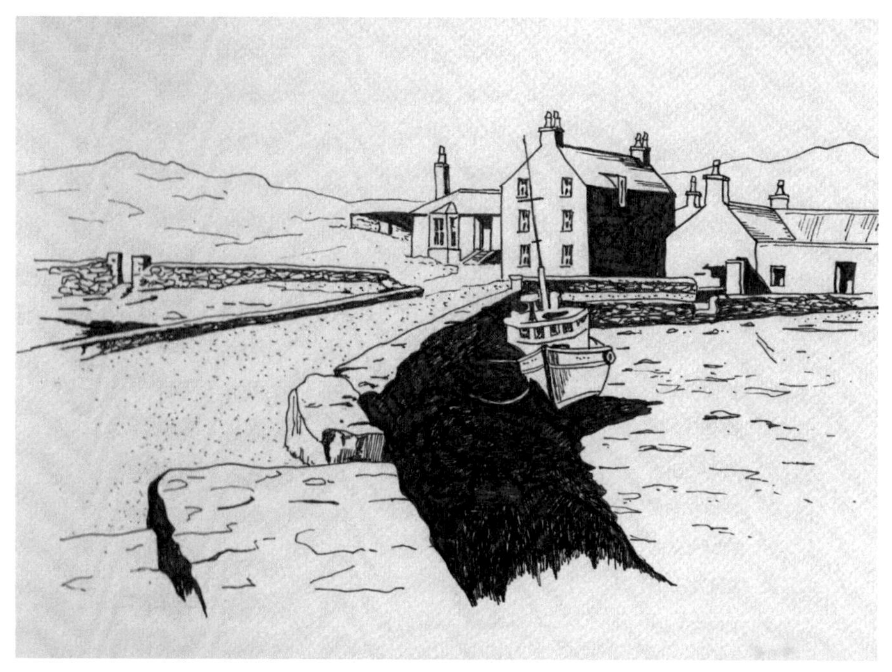

Rodel harbour.

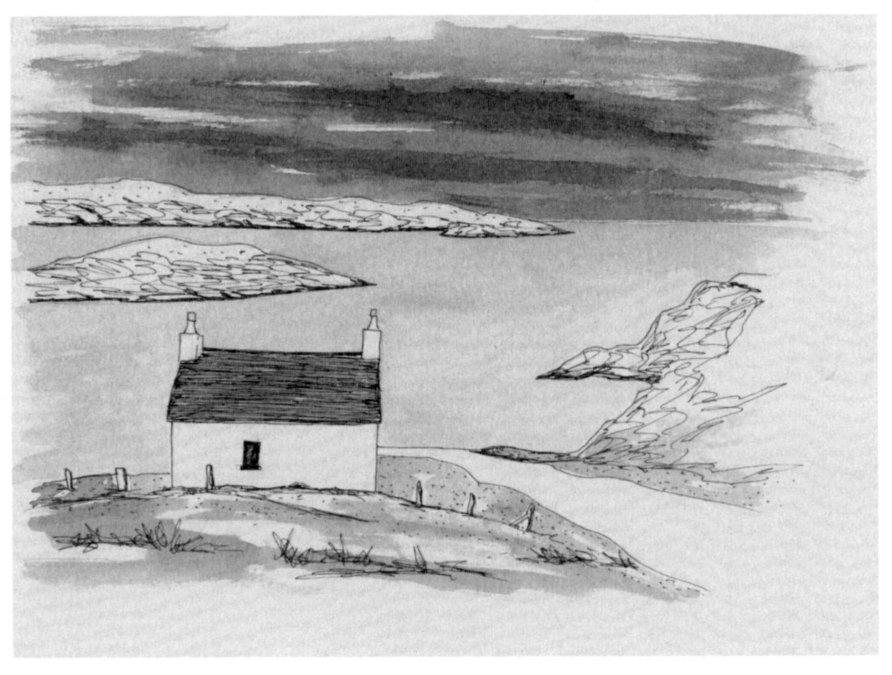

Rodel croft.

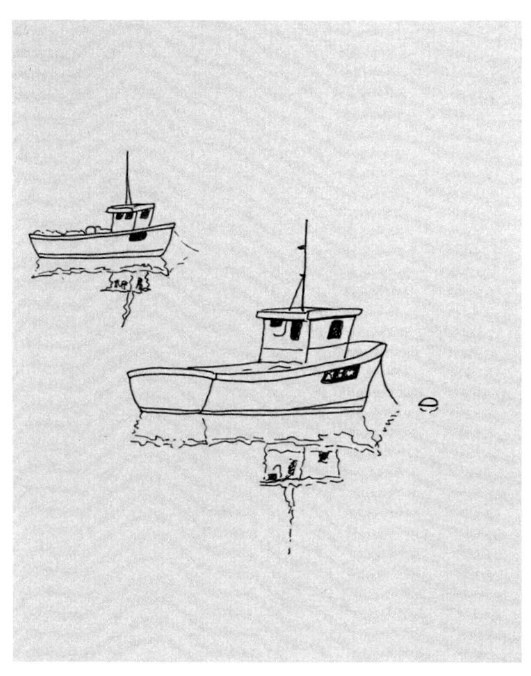

Boats, Rodel.

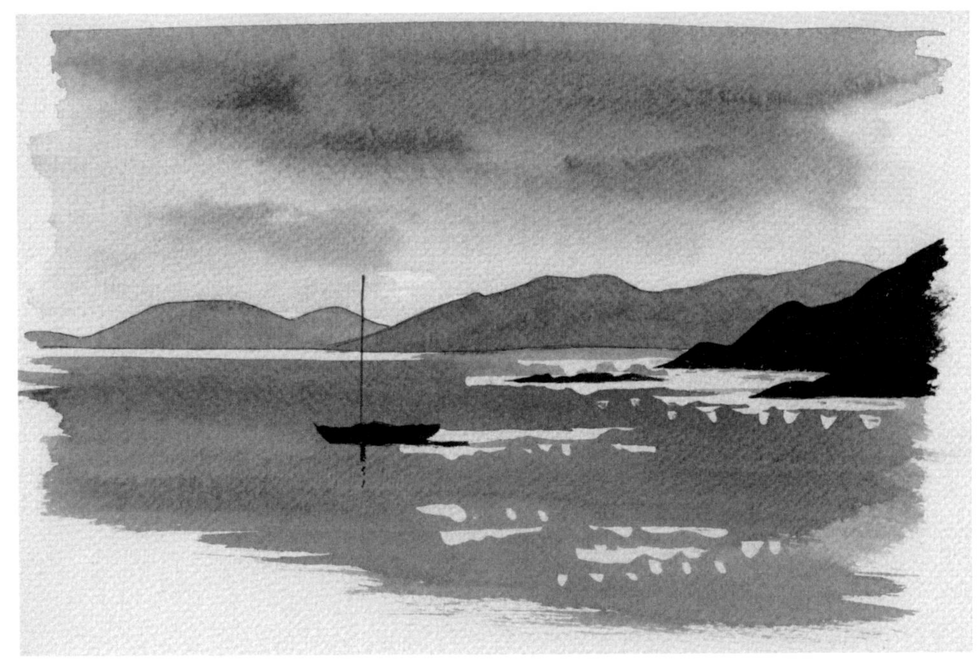

Safe mooring, Rodel.

Luath Press Limited

committed to publishing well written books worth reading

LUATH PRESS takes its name from Robert Burns, whose little collie Luath (*Gael.*, swift or nimble) tripped up Jean Armour at a wedding and gave him the chance to speak to the woman who was to be his wife and the abiding love of his life. Burns called one of the 'Twa Dogs' Luath after Cuchullin's hunting dog in Ossian's *Fingal*. Luath Press was established in 1981 in the heart of Burns country, and is now based a few steps up the road from Burns' first lodgings on Edinburgh's Royal Mile.
Luath offers you distinctive writing with a hint of unexpected pleasures.
Most bookshops in the UK, the US, Canada, Australia, New Zealand and parts of Europe, either carry our books in stock or can order them for you.
To order direct from us, please send a £sterling cheque, postal order, international money order or your credit card details (number, address of cardholder and expiry date) to us at the address below. Please add post and packing as follows:
UK – £1.00 per delivery address; overseas surface mail – £2.50 per delivery address; overseas airmail – £3.50 for the first book to each delivery address, plus £1.00 for each additional book by airmail to the same address. If your order is a gift, we will happily enclose your card or message at no extra charge.

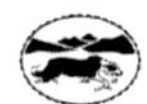

Luath Press Limited
543/2 Castlehill
The Royal Mile
Edinburgh EH1 2ND
Scotland
Telephone: +44 (0)131 225 4326 (24 hours)
Email: sales@luath.co.uk
Website: www.luath.co.uk